the naturally scented home

the naturally

scented home

JULIA BIRD

Text by **Emma Warlow** Photographs by **Debi Treloar**

First published in Great Britain in 2000 by
Collins & Brown Limited
London House, Great Eastern Wharf
Parkgate Road, London SW11 4NQ

Distributed In the United States and Canada by Sterling Publishing
Company, 387 Park Avenue South, New York, NY 10016, USA

British Library Cataloguing-in-Publication Data:
A catalogue record for this title is available from the British Library.
9 8 7 6 5 4 3 2 1
ISBN 185585 797 9

A BERRY BOOK
Conceived, edited and designed by Susan Berry for Collins & Brown
Designer: Debbie Mole
Editor: Judy Spours
The author and publisher cannot be held responsible for misadventure
resulting from the misuse of essential oils, or any other technique
in this book.

Reproduction by Classic Scan, Singapore
Printed and bound in Hong Kong

contents

introduction

HOME FRAGRANCING IS ENJOYING an extraordinary renaissance. Scented candles, pot pourri, fragranced laundry sprays, aromatherapy oils, incense — all kinds of perfume for the environment are available in most high streets. Even the supermarket chains have jumped on the bandwagon — while you shop for food for your dinner party, you can think about shopping for its mood as well. There's simply no excuse not to fill your home with scent.

So why do it? Where did the vogue come from? At its simplest level, it's a symptom of our national obsession with all things related to the home, the ultimate final touch in a carefully planned interior, like the right designer fragrance for our fashionably-clad bodies. It also has practical, hygiene-driven appeal; masking unpleasant smells with delicious ones has been a function of perfume throughout history.

But beyond all that, and the reason for its broadening appeal, is the fact that fragrance has the power to bring sensual pleasure into our lives. Air-conditioning, pollution, fluorescent lighting, computer screens and traffic noise are facts of modern life we have learned to accept, but restoring our spirits in the wake of their onslaught has become something of a priority. Indulging our sense of smell has a powerfully therapeutic effect, intensifying our enjoyment of everything we do. A bath scented with favourite essential oils becomes an oasis of calm; a glass of wine sipped on a summer's evening surrounded by the heady sweetness of jasmine tastes like nectar; an open fire takes on a further comforting dimension if you burn applewood or pine cones. Even listening to music has a new intensity when you're relaxing in a darkened room filled with the subtle aromas of scented candles or incense.

The naturally scented home is inevitably one that looks to the past for its inspiration. Going back to first principles brings us to the core necessities of domestic life, things that have remained unchanged for centuries. Paradoxically, this ethos is as cutting-edge as it can be: minimal, pure

OPPOSITE: *The simplest way to fragrance your home is to bring fresh flowers into as many rooms as possible. You needn't be extravagant — the perfume of a single lily is so intense that it can fill even large spaces like hallways or landings with its exotically sweet scent.*

and essential. Contemporary home style uses the raw materials of the past — stone flagstones, natural floorcoverings, wood, furnishings in wool, linen, silk and cotton — that appeal to some indefinable instinct. People have been surrounded with these materials for centuries, yet in the twenty-first they are as relevant and enjoyable as ever.

Our sense of smell is our most powerful, developed when it was the key to everyday survival. Anatomically it connects directly with the limbic system, which is the seat of emotion and memory. Smells are loaded with emotional resonance and able to trigger an instant memory of events, people and places we may have thought were forgotten — the famous Proustian rush of recognition. Mediterranean holiday memories flood back when you inhale the dry scent of rosemary and thyme or the delicious pungent spice of a torn basil leaf. The powdery warmth of vanilla comforts the senses with its connotations of home-baking and baby powder. The unmistakable combination of resinous pine and orange evokes all the sensual delights of Christmas.

Without our sense of smell, food and drink would be tasteless, without nuance. Wine, for instance, is not described as having 'a good nose' for nothing; remove our ability to smell while we drink and we will hardly taste it at all. Scientific research has shown just how powerful scent is in all personal relationships, too. We are instinctively drawn to those people whose smell we find attractive, even if this might be the very last factor we would consciously admit to!

Getting in touch with this subconscious power is what this book is about. We hope it prompts a new appreciation of the natural fragrances we enjoy simply in passing — the honeyed drift of beeswax that lingers in the air when a candle is snuffed out; the rush of summer scent we inhale when lawns are cut; the oaky dampness of a recently drawn cork — as well as inspiring a new approach to cosmetic perfumes. Using fragrance in all its forms to enhance the way we live has its roots in prehistory, so there's nothing revolutionary here. We hope simply to inspire renewed respect for traditional wisdom and techniques, and to show how effective and relevant they are today. Bringing the pleasures of scent into every corner of your home couldn't be simpler.

OPPOSITE: *Some spices, like star anise, are so strongly aromatic that simply leaving them in open containers around the house will allow their fragrance to diffuse through the air.*

CHAPTER 1

FIRST PRINCIPLES

first principles

OPPOSITE: *Turning your home into a naturally scented haven will take some time, trouble and preparation. Build up a range of airtight containers, attractive storage jars (made of both dark and clear glass) and spray bottles to facilitate the creation of your own fragrant mixtures. Recycling comes into its own here — new life starts for old favourites from the kitchen and bathroom.*

THE BEAUTY OF USING SIMPLE, natural products to bring fragrance into your home is that you will probably already have most of the necessary materials in your kitchen cupboards. There are a few pieces of more specialist equipment that you will need to invest in, but most of the ideas described throughout this book are kept deliberately basic and accessible.

Many of the ingredients used will likewise be staples of your store cupboard and garden. Clearly it makes sense to keep equipment, ingredients and completed recipes safely out of the reach of children and animals. Designate one locked cupboard, or a high open shelf as your 'fragrant zone' — a capsule version of the more extensive Elizabethan still-room. Have fun with the packaging and presentation of your work. Recycle attractive bottles, tins and boxes; save remnants of favourite fabrics and trimmings for really individual bags and sachets; attach hand-written labels with gold thread or fine fuse wire, or string.

you will need

- Pestle and mortar
- Bain-marie or double boiler for melting wax/soap flakes
- Airtight containers for storing spices and dried herbs and flowers — and completed pot pourri recipes and the like

- Dark glass bottles for combining and storing essential and carrier oils
- Pipette
- Scales and measuring jugs
- Measuring spoons
- Chopping boards and knives
- Mixing bowls

- Wooden spoons
- Funnel
- Filter papers and holder
- Muslin or cloths
- Kitchen towel
- Scissors and secateurs
- Plastic and glass spray bottles or atomizers

- String
- Blotting paper
- Sticky or tie-on labels
- Sewing materials
- Burner or vaporizer for diffusing essential oils
- Small, open, heatproof dishes for burning incense

essential oils

ESSENTIAL OILS HAVE BEEN at the heart of perfumery from its earliest days and, while chemical imitations have begun to dominate the commercial perfume market, these powerful, fragrant distillations of plants (literally their very essence) open up a world of fragrancing possibilities at home. The undeniably therapeutic properties of many adds a further dimension to their use. The subconscious responses we have to smell can be targeted using the appropriate oils to promote relaxation, alertness, confidence, serenity — whatever mood you seek to inspire. Additionally, many oils have overtly antiseptic, antiviral properties that make them perfect for use in kitchens and bathrooms, where hygiene can be achieved without the strong smell of disinfectant.

The oils are sold in small, dark-coloured glass bottles, with integral droppers. They can be used for massage, diluted in a light carrier oil, such as almond, grape-seed or jojoba, or in bathing water or water sprays. They can be vaporized over a heat source — ceramic or metal rings, for instance, are sold to sit over light bulbs and drops of diluted oil in the rings evaporate as the bulb heats up. You can drop the oils directly on to a cool light bulb before switching a light on, but some oils are quite viscous and things can get a bit sticky. A conventional burner, usually ceramic or earthenware, allows a dilution of oils to be warmed in an integral dish above a burning tea-light, while the electrical variety gently diffuses oils from its wide reservoir. Experiment with different combinations to find the marriage of oils you like best; once you find it, you have a signature fragrance for the home. The combination guides available with most oils make a good starting-point and common sense — and your nose — will tell you when a mix is unlikely to succeed.

OPPOSITE: *Essential oils are probably the most important factor in creating a naturally scented home environment. They smell intensely delicious and they can soothe, refresh, stimulate and heal. Many have crucial antiseptic and anti-bacterial properties — and a little bottle goes a long long way.*

The oils are highly concentrated and should almost never be used on the skin if they are undiluted by either oil or water. The most notable exception to this rule is lavender, whose anti-inflammatory, healing properties were officially endorsed by the French chemist René Gattefosse, who plunged his burned hand into what he thought was a beaker of water, but was in fact lavender oil. The speed of healing and absence of scarring he observed inspired further successful experimentation into other essential oils and the term 'aromatherapy' was born. In the light of current interest in all things alternative, organic and natural, the word is cynically paraded by makers of everything from scented candles and bath oils to face packs and shampoos without much authority, and has become debased as a result. True aromatherapy is an important area of complementary medicine that harnesses the psychological, physiological and pharmacological effects of essential oils. Although the subject cannot be pursued in depth here, suffice to say that the pleasure of smelling these oils is underlined with their positive therapeutic benefits and that their use should be tailored to the varying functions of different rooms.

As you browse along the densely packed shelves of oils in a health shop or herbal suppliers, spare a thought for the house-wives of old who had to labour away in their still-rooms for weeks to distill such a range of precious oils.

BASIL
Scent: clear, sweet, spicy
Properties: great against headaches; uplifting; aids concentration; anti-insect
Blends with: bergamot, geranium

BENZOIN
Scent: sweet, tingling, vanilla-like
Properties: comforting and calming; clears airways; fixative
Blends with: rose, sandalwood

BERGAMOT
Scent: light, citrus, floral, refreshing
Properties: sedative, yet uplifting; antiseptic; anti-insect and keeps pets off plants
Blends with: cypress, jasmine, lavender, neroli

CEDARWOOD
Scent: dry, woody, warm
Properties: calming and soothing; moths hate it
Blends with: cypress, juniper, rose

CAMOMILE
Scent: floral, apple-toned, fresh
Properties: relaxing, calming and great for insomnia
Blends with: geranium, lavender, rose, patchouli

CINNAMON
Scent: sweet, musky, spicy
Properties: antiseptic; restorative; aphrodisiac
Blends with: best alone

CITRONELLA
Scent: strong, antiseptic, lemon
Properties: clears mind and uplifts spirit; effective anti-insect used in sprays, candles or on cotton wool balls inside storage chests
Blends with: lavender

CLARY SAGE
Scent: nutty, rich, grassy
Properties: relaxing, euphoria-inducing
Blends with: cedarwood, geranium, juniper, lavender, sandalwood

CLOVE
Scent: penetrating, heavy, spicy
Properties: analgesic; stimulating and uplifting; disinfectant; anti-insect; aphrodisiac
Blends with: best alone

CYPRESS
Scent: spicy, woody, refreshing
Properties: calming, diffuses feelings of anger; antiseptic; anti-insect
Blends with: juniper, rosemary, pine, sandalwood

EUCALYPTUS
Scent: clear, penetrating
Properties: antiseptic; antiviral; kills bacteria; clears respiratory problems; stimulating and cooling
Blends with: lavender, rosemary, pine

FRANKINCENSE
Scent: woody, spicy, citrus
Properties: soothing, uplifting effect; clears airways; anti-inflammatory
Blends with: basil, cypress, lavender, myrrh, patchouli, sandalwood

GERANIUM
Scent: heavy, floral, rose-like
Properties: tonic to the spirits; antidepressant; anti-insect
Blends with: most oils

GRAPEFRUIT
Scent: sharp, refreshing
Properties: antidepressant and combats stress; stimulating; relieves headache
Blends with: lemon, lavender, orange, rosemary

JASMINE
Scent: heady, sweet, floral
Properties: promotes feelings of positivity; revitalizing; aphrodisiac
Blends with: most oils

JUNIPER
Scent: refreshing, woody
Properties: antiseptic; disinfecting; stimulates and strengthens the spirit
Blends with: cypress, citrus oils, lavender, pine

LAVENDER
Scent: sweet, powdery, penetrating, woody
Properties: king of oils with a range of uses — relaxing; antiseptic; anti-insect; antidepressant; anti-bacterial
Blends with: most oils

LEMON
Scent: bright, fresh, sharp
Properties: stimulating and refreshing; antiseptic; anti-insect
Blends with: orange, lavender, rosemary

LEMONGRASS
Scent: sweet, lemony
Properties: stimulating and energizing; strong antiseptic; anti-insect
Blends with: citrus oils, lavender

LIME
Scent: sharp, bitter, citrus
Properties: uplifting and cooling; antiseptic; antiviral; kills bacteria
Blends with: lemon, grapefruit, lavender

MARJORAM
Scent: warm, spicy, herbal
Properties: calming; comforting; aphrodisiac
Blends with: bergamot, lavender

MELISSA
Scent: sweet, floral, lemon (the herb is also known as LEMON BALM)
Properties: antidepressant; promotes positivity; anti-insect
Blends with: geranium, lavender, petitgrain, ylang ylang

NEROLI
Scent: heady, floral, exquisite
Properties: antidepressant; promotes relaxation and euphoria; aphrodisiac; kills bacteria
Blends with: most oils

ORANGE
Scent: warm, fruity, refreshing
Properties: cheering; refreshing; relieves tension; antiseptic
Blends with: lavender, benzoin

PATCHOULI
Scent: rich, sweet, spicy, pungent
Properties: antidepressant; balancing; aphrodisiac; anti-insect; fixative
Blends with: most oils

PEPPERMINT
Scent: clear, penetrating, sweet
Properties: cooling and clearing; stimulating; anti-insect and anti-vermin
Blends with: benzoin, lavender, rosemary

PETITGRAIN
Scent: floral, citrus, woody
Properties: calming and reassuring; antidepressant
Blends with: most oils

PINE
Scent: fresh, woody, clean
Properties: refreshing; stimulating; antiseptic; disinfecting
Blends with: cedarwood, eucalyptus, rosemary, sage

ROSE
Scent: pungent, floral, exquisite, very feminine
Properties: soothing; aphrodisiac; antiseptic
Blends with: most oils

ROSEMARY
Scent: strong, refreshing, herbal
Properties: stimulating; energizing; antiseptic
Blends with: basil, bergamot, lavender, peppermint

SANDALWOOD
Scent: exotic, woody, masculine
Properties: deeply relaxing and comforting; aphrodisiac
Blends with: benzoin, rose, neroli, petitgrain

TEA TREE
Scent: fresh, pungent, minty
Properties: antiseptic; antibiotic; kills bacteria; stimulating
Blends with: best alone

THYME
Scent: warm, pungent, green
Properties: antiseptic; kills bacteria; reviving and stimulating
Blends with: bergamot, petitgrain, rosemary

YLANG YLANG
Scent: heavy, floral, heady, exotic
Properties: antidepressant; promotes joy; aphrodisiac
Blends with: jasmine, neroli, rose, sandalwood

essential spices

CARDAMOM, CINNAMON, CLOVES, nutmeg, star anise — the very names transport us to the distant lands that are their home. Spices have been staples of oriental and Asian cuisine since ancient times and their export to the West opened the map of the world. Spices came to Europe from Arabia, Africa and the Ottoman empire along the ancient caravan routes. These extraordinary seeds, roots, barks and powders had the ability to enliven a very bland medieval diet, preserve food and disguise any that was less than fresh, and inevitably provoked huge commercial interest.

In addition to their indubitable contributions to our diets — where would we be without black pepper? — the smell of spices, like that of herbs, has always been a crucial part of their popularity. Chinese courtiers at the Imperial palaces chewed cloves, for instance, not for their personal pleasure but so that their breath would be fragrant for the Emperor's greater convenience. Interestingly, clove oil has long been recognized as a powerful analgesic for toothache, so perhaps there was another motive for this habit. The tantalizing aroma of curries cooking — whether it's the darker scent of cumin and tamarind or the delicacy of cardamom and lemongrass — works powerfully on the imagination. The addition of nutmeg, cloves and cinnamon to apple dishes has rendered a pie made without the assistance of at least one of the three a pale, scentless substitute.

Harnessing the wealth of spicy scents to fragrance your home brings a particular warmth to the environment. Spices complement the floral and herbal elements in scented sachets or pot pourris — cloves with rose and sandalwood and cardamom with lavender and lemon, for example. And festive combinations of pine needles or bay leaves with the richness of cinnamon and nutmeg are bewitching.

CARDAMOM
(Elettaria cardamomum)
Grown in southern India; seeds are strongly pungent, rich and warming; staple of Indian cookery and used by Arabs to flavour coffee; good in spiced wine and with stewed fruit; brought to England by the Normans; said to aid digestion and sweeten the breath

CINNAMON
(Cinnamomum verum)
Native of Sri Lanka, cultivated in West Indies and eastern countries; finest quality pale bark is harvested from young shoots; sweet, delicate flavour; said to be stimulant, aid digestion and be antiseptic

CLOVE
(Syzygium aromaticum)
Native of Molucca islands, cultivated in Zanzibar; listed in early Chinese herbals and well-known in Classical Europe, but rare in England until Norman invasion; flower buds harvested and dried until they turn brown; very strong, unmistakable scent, warming and aromatic, antiseptic

GINGER

(Zingiber officinale)

Native of south-east Asian rain forests, cultivated in West Indies; rhizome is used fresh, dried, tinned, ground or preserved and is essential to Eastern cuisine; introduced to northern Europe by Romans and became staple of medieval cookery; warm, sweet, stimulating and soothing for colds and coughs

NUTMEG AND MACE

(Myristica fragrans)

Native of Molucca islands, cultivated in West Indies and tropical countries; seed is the nutmeg, protected by red fleshy network — the mace; nutmeg and mace dried separately; store nutmegs whole and grate when needed; dried blades of mace are available to use whole; mace has more powerful aroma than nutmeg; nutmeg is calming and aids digestion

LEFT: *The shapes and colours of spices are immediately evocative — bringing the East powerfully to mind.*

PEPPER

(Piper nigrum)

Native of India and Asia, cultivated in other tropical countries; black peppercorns are the vine's dried red berries; most popular spice in Europe since Roman times; hot, pungent aroma useful in sweet and savoury dishes

STAR ANISE

(Illicium verum)

Native of south west China; tree has large star-shaped fruits, each point containing a seed; stores very well and a little goes a long way; sweet, sour aroma reminiscent of aniseed; warm, stimulating

VANILLA

(Vanilla planifolia)

Native of South America, cultivated in other tropical countries; climbing plant produces long, yellow-green pods that are picked unripe and cured until dark brown and sticky to the touch; delicious, amber-like scent is very intense — a single pod will scent a whole jar of sugar for a year or more

essential herbs

LIFE WITHOUT HERBS is hard to imagine, so essential have they become to the full enjoyment of food. The simple addition of a single bay leaf to a stew, of chopped parsley to a white sauce, or of a bunch of rosemary to roasting lamb, revolutionizes the flavour, turning basic food into gourmet fare. The powerful therapeutic properties of many herbs have made them invaluable in natural medicine for centuries, and everybody can enjoy the soothing benefits of camomile, marjoram or lemon verbena teas, for example. A garden without a plot — or at least a few pots — devoted to the cultivation of herbs is deprived not only of valuable cooking ingredients, but also of a range of really attractive, useful, hardy plants. Think of incorporating lavender bushes, rosemary, bay trees, flowering thyme, feathery parsley and giant fennel into your planting. And you could also try delicate tarragon, velvety sage, brilliant blue-flowered borage and the pink stars held aloft by fragile chives. Given partial sun and well-drained soil, these everyday herbs thrive anywhere — mint needs no excuse to invade and take over a garden — and the less hardy varieties, like the different basils and coriander, will do well in window boxes or even grown inside, benefiting from the warmth of the house.

Aromatic quality is, of course, the key to the enduring charm of these plants. Just to touch them is to release fabulous scent into the air — try brushing past lavender bushes in full bloom or walking across a camomile lawn — and bringing them into the home to enjoy is a natural extension of that pleasure. Strewing sweet rush and tansy on the floor was a medieval practise informed both by a need for comfort — the layers of grasses and herbs softened the impact of stone and wooden flooring — and to overcome unsavoury smells, which were thought to

OPPOSITE: *Herbs delight us with their fragrance, their taste and their good looks — the soft, feathery fronds of dill and tansy; the velvety tongues of mint and sage; the sculptural spines of rosemary; the tangled stems of thyme; and the bobbing flowerheads of chives.*

carry disease. The faith in many herbs' ability to cleanse with their scent was not entirely misplaced, since it has since been established that oils from thyme, lavender, rosemary and juniper, for instance, are all powerful natural antiseptics. Posies made up of tansy, rosemary and lavender were carried in the sixteenth century and in later centuries to ward off disease and to sweeten the passage of the bearer through the streets — and had the added advantage of being a pleasure to carry.

Folkloric associations with certain herbs, made familiar through the writings of Shakespeare and other contemporaneous poets, influenced the later Victorian love of creating messages in the form of floral bouquets. Hops and valerian were traditionally, and correctly, linked to sleep; anything sweet-smelling was considered to be an aphrodisiac; and rosemary was, of course, for remembrance. Chervil represented sincerity; rue was said to indicate disdain; lemon balm was invoked to indicate sympathy; the fresh smell of mint signified purity; and parsley was considered a festive herb. Including herbs in bouquets is still a lovely idea, and sometimes herbs alone make enough of a statement. Sadly, we have now lost much of our immediate knowledge of folklore, and it may be as well to attach attractive handmade labels to bouquets to spell out the messages that you wish to convey through the herbs.

ANGELICA

(Angelica archangelica)
Monumental, with large, glossy green leaves, hollow ridged stem, sweet-smelling yellow-green flowers borne on large nectar-sticky umbels. Used for candied cake decoration, but also for flavouring fish dishes and sweetening stewed fruit. Infused dried leaves taste like China tea. Dried leaves also used in pot pourri. Effective tonic, stimulant and expectorant

BASIL

(Ocimum basilicum)
Tender annual that enjoys sun and warmth. Broad, juicy leaves with delicious spicy aroma are invaluable addition to salads and in cooking. Strong tonic, antiseptic, stimulatant, digestive. Traditional strewing herb, deters flies

BAY

(Laurus nobilis)
Strong, shiny evergreen leaves and small greenish-yellow flowers in spring that develop into black berries. Aromatic fresh or dried leaves used as flavouring in food. Antiseptic and preservative (burned with juniper against the plague)

BERGAMOT

(Monarda didyama)
Native of North America but widely grown today. Tall, with toothed, highly scented leaves, shaggy scarlet flowers. Fresh leaves good in salads and summer drinks; dried leaves make aromatic tisane reminiscent of scented China tea (Earl Grey tea is scented with bergamot)

CAMOMILE

(Chamomaemelum nobile — Roman, and Chamomilla recutita — German)
Roman camomile is grown as turf for scented lawns, and bears aromatic white and yellow flowers. German camomile is a straggly upright plant with similar flowers of white petals around a yellow centre. Both used for tisanes — to soothe digestion, heal inflammation, aid sleep and as a rinse to lighten fair hair. Antiseptic and healing — traditional strewing herb

CORIANDER

(Coriandrum sativum)
Soft, parsley-like leaves and pungent, sweetish smell. Fresh leaves good foil to chilli dishes and in salads; aromatic, sweet seeds also useful as a flavouring. Stimulant and digestive

EUCALYPTUS

(Eucalyptus globulus)

Australian but cultivated worldwide. Young leaves are rounded, blue-tinged with silvery bloom; older ones pointed and glossy green. Antiseptic and disinfectant, expectorant

GARLIC

(Allium sativum)

Unmistakable aroma; heightens flavour when used sparingly in cooking, very pungent if used raw. Antiseptic, tonic and useful against colds

HOP

(Humulus lupulus)

Climbing fibrous stems bearing pale rough leaves; female flowers become papery cones with valuable properties. Used in brewing, as a preservative, to leaven bread, as digestive and appetite stimulant, and to promote sleep

JUNIPER

(Juniperus communis)

Shrubby plant with sharp, grey-green leaves and aromatic scent. Dried, blue-black berries add to flavour of game dishes; bruise before use. Leaves and woody stems add fragrance to fires. Antiseptic (branches burned as fumigant in times of plague)

LAVENDER

(Lavandula angustifolia)

Shrubby plant with narrow, greyish-green leaves and mauvish-blue flowers held on long stems. Antiseptic, disinfecting and insecticide properties have made lavender a mainstay of domestic practise since classical times, and its glorious, intense scent has dominated perfumery for just as long

LEMON BALM

(Melissa officinalis)

Green nettle-like leaves and creamy flowers. Minty-lemon scented leaves make delicious tisanes — soothing and refreshing to drink, or add to the bath for comforting soak. Antiseptic

LEMON VERBENA

(Lippia citriodora)

Graceful shrub with sweet, lemon-scented leaves and pale lilac flowers in late summer. Leaves retain flavour and aroma well — use for tisanes or in pot pourri and scented sachets

MARIGOLD

(Calendula officinalis)

Orange, daisy-like heads (edible petals), downy stems and long rounded leaves. Stimulant and soothing, healing to skin

MARJORAM

(Origanum majorana)

Sweet, warming aromatic herb with fine reddish stem and small grey-green leaves. Used as subtle flavouring in cooking and in sweet pot pourris. Soothing, antiseptic, digestive. Traditional strewing herb.

MINT

(Mentha spicata — spearmint; Mentha x piperita — peppermint; Mentha suaveolens — applemint; Mentha x gentilis — ginger mint; Mentha pulegium — pennyroyal)

Huge family of plants, all bearing small flowers in midsummer and pungent leaves. Delicious addition to cooking and salads, and a cooling, refreshing tisane. Antiseptic, digestive, uplifting. Pennyroyal used against fleas

ORRIS

(Iris fiorentina)

White-flowered iris with strongly violet-scented rhizome. Powder from orris root used as fixative; oil used for violet scents in perfume industry

PARSLEY

(Petroselinum crispum)

Curly-leaved, universally useful herb, indispensable in cooking. Breath freshener against garlic. Tonic, digestive, anti-inflammatory

ROSE-SCENTED GERANIUM

(Pelargonium graveolens)

Most popular of large pelargonium family, which includes lemon, nutmeg and peppermint scents. Tall with fragrant leaves and small mauve or pink flower clusters. Flavouring for sweet cakes and puddings and dried in pot pourri

ROSEMARY

(Rosmarinus officinalis)

Hardy evergreen with woody stem, spiny leaves and pale indigo flowers in summer. Strongly aromatic role in cooking. Antiseptic, stimulating, warming. Traditionally burned against infection and laid among linen

RUE

(Ruta graveolens)

Evergreen with round, soft, bluish leaves. Can irritate the skin. Antiseptic, insecticide and the herb of repentance as twigs were used traditionally to sprinkle holy water during Mass

SAGE

(Salvia officinalis)

Shrubby, woody plant with long, velvety, grey-green leaves. Strong, dry aroma; used in cookery to balance fatty foods like pork, goose, cheeses. Astringent, tonic, stimulant. Burned as a fumigant

SOUTHERNWOOD

(Artemisia abrotanum)

Feathery, soft, grey-green leaves with sweet penetrating smell; tiny yellow button-like flowers. Strongly antiseptic (carried to ward off plague) and deterrent to moths.

TANSY

(Tanacetum vulgare)

Dark, feathery, aromatic leaves and little button-like yellow flowerheads. Insecticide, disinfectant. Traditional strewing herb

THYME

(Thymus vulgaris)

Shrubby, woody herb with tendrils bearing small, oval leaves and pale mauve or white flowers in summer. Vital element of Mediterranean cookery; very good dried herb. Strong antiseptic, tonic, stimulant

WOODRUFF

(Galium odoratum)

Smooth dark-green leaves and star-shaped white flowers. Valued for its sweet smell, which intensifies on drying

CHAPTER 2

THE KITCHEN

IF HOME IS, as the old saying has it, where the heart is, then the heart of any home is its kitchen. The combined associations of those twin necessities, fire and food, draw us inexorably towards the kitchen, as if for comfort. People at parties retreat into kitchens because they offer a refuge from the challenge of social intercourse. Kitchens are centres of creativity and activity, utilitarian yet welcoming and the focus of family life. But most of all, of course, they are about food.

the smell of food

KITCHENS ARE THE SOURCE of the most delicious smells in the house. If you had to list your favourites, the chances are that many would have kitchen associations. Those of frying bacon, onions or garlic sizzling in olive oil, freshly ground coffee, baking bread, apples stewing with cinnamon; torn mint and basil, lemon zest — the list goes on. Cooking has its own aromatic rewards and a busy kitchen will be filled with a panoply of tantalizing smells day by day. The herbs and spices that supplement the delicious fragrance of more basic ingredients bring extra pleasure. Think of the rush of saliva prompted by the smell of curry cooking, as the exotic spices slowly and aromatically combine with meat and vegetables. Pop a vanilla pod or layers of rose petals into your sugar jar and fragrance will explode every time you open it.

I remember my mother making Turkish coffee as a special treat, perhaps to finish off an eastern meal she had cooked for us. It was always served in a traditional copper coffee set with tiny cups filled with the strong, sweet and deliciously aromatic coffee. Place one tablespoon per person of very finely ground Turkish coffee into a pan and an equal amount of sugar. Add one cardamom pod (optional) and one espresso coffee cup of water per person. Bring to the boil, and as it rises up, take it off the heat immediately. Re-boil in this way four times if you are making for four people. Add one teaspoon of rose water. Pour into espresso coffee cups.

LEFT: A kitchen without spices is deprived of the world's most aromatic culinary sensations. Adding even the smallest amount of spice, whether it is cumin, turmeric, coriander or cardamom, revoultionizes the flavour of food.

BELOW: The kitchen is the domain of nature's most tantalizing smells, like the unmistakable aroma of onions and garlic.

recipe:
spiced hot
chocolate

A bowl of hot chocolate spiced with cinnamon, nutmeg and cardamom has an irresistible aroma.

Add a small stick of cinnamon, a little grated nutmeg and 3 cardamom pods to 600 ml (1 pint) of milk. Warm very gently, taking off the heat just before it boils. Leave to infuse for 5 minutes. Remove cinnamon and cardamom pods and add grated chocolate. Stir until melted over a gentle heat. Pour into bowls and top with whipped cream and a sprinkling of grated chocolate.

recipe:pesto

A dynamic sauce saturated with aromatic herbs that can be used to dress pasta, salads, soups and casseroles.

- 2 handfuls of basil (or coriander, tarragon, rocket or parsley — whichever you prefer)
- 3 cloves of garlic
- 2 tablespoons pine nuts
- 2 tablespoons grated parmesan cheese
- 2 tablespoons olive oil

Pound garlic in a pestle and mortar (or electric grinder), add pine nuts and herb to make a thick paste. Stir in the parmesan and gradually add the olive oil. Decant into a jar, adding a little more olive oil on top. This will keep in the fridge for a few days.

kitchen herbs

THE SIMPLE PRESENCE OF FRESH or even dried herbs in the kitchen serves as a permanent source of gentle ambient fragrance. You really don't need a herb garden to grow and enjoy herbs. Pots clustered along a sunny window-sill bring the individual power of each fragrance to the nose with surprising vividness, and picking a sprig or two releases even more of the aroma. Herbs to try for maximum sensory impact include basil, mint, rosemary, chives, tarragon and thyme.

Happily, the herbs that smell thrilling are also the most rewarding to use in cooking. Fresh herbs such as mint, lemon verbena and camomile make delicious, sweet-smelling tisanes when steeped in boiling water for a few minutes. Sprigs of fresh rosemary or a bunch of thyme can be popped into the pot, around a roasting leg of lamb or beneath the skin of a plump Sunday chicken. Nothing could be more tantalizing than the smell of baking bread when there are herbs in the dough. Make a habit of using fragrant herbs in your cooking, and more especially in your fresh salads, where their form and pungence is at its most dramatic, and the very act of making dinner will perfume the air.

LEFT: *The intense green of basil, coriander or tarragon pesto makes it a pleasure to behold, and it is full of the fresh aroma of the herbs.*

RIGHT: *Adding strongly aromatic dried herbs, such as rosemary, to your bread gives it a whole new personality, each slice bringing with it a breath of the Mediterranean. Offering herb bread with a simple supper of soup or an omelette turns the occasion into a special meal.*

one

two

three

Culinary Herb Wreath

you will need

- Medium gauge wire. You will need about 4 circles of wire — about 60 cm (2 ft) in diameter. Two lengths of wire approx. 1.5 m (5 ft) long to hang wreath. (Alternatively, buy a ready-made florist's wreath base.)
- Roll of gardener's green-coated wire
- Wire cutters
- Cup hook
- String
- Large bundle of bay leaves
- Gardener's shears or kitchen scissors

HERBS ARE wonderfully decorative in their natural state, but work brilliantly when woven on wire frames to make wreaths. Bay leaves lend themselves well to wreath-making, thanks to their strength and size, but experiment with other herbs you might have in abundance. We rang the changes by hanging our wreath horizontally and adorning it with parcels of culinary herbs to serve as bouquets garnis. Choose herbs that you use regularly — bigger bunches of rosemary for roast meats and smaller mixed bouquets for soups and omelettes. Hanging homemade bouquets garnis on a bought wreath is a good compromise for those not confident enough to tackle one from scratch.

method

one Cut 4 circles of wire about 60 cm (2 ft) in diameter. Bind the four thicknesses together with gardener's coated wire, starting at the two cut ends.

two Cut smallish sprigs of bay and bind onto the circle using small lengths of gardener's wire. Continue until you have a full and equal bushy effect. To hang from the ceiling, cut two lengths of wire, attach at four points around the wreath and simply hook them at the top onto a cup hook secured into the ceiling.

three Finally, cut lengths of string approximately 25 cm (10 in) long. Cut small bunches of herbs and loosely tie them with a simple knot (so they are easy to undo) at intervals around the wreath. You will probably find it easier to tie the herb bouquets onto the wreath when it is hanging.

RIGHT: *Making fragrant herbal teas using mint, camomile or lemon verbena — fresh herbs if you have them — fills the kitchen with delicate scents. The cleansing taste and positive effects on your health are additional advantages! Add a little honey if you prefer a sweeter drink.*

OPPOSITE: *Sugar can be easily scented by layering it with fragrant ingredients, such as lavender, orange peel, rose petals, or these rose-scented geranium leaves, in a large jar. A pod of vanilla will do the job well, too.*

tisanes

ALMOST ANY HERB can be steeped in boiling water to make a delicious therapeutic alternative to coffee or ordinary tea. The medicinal properties of the herbs will result in a soothing, stimulating or relaxing effect. Add ½ litre (1 pint) of boiling water (mineral water is preferable) to a good tablespoon of the fresh herb (or 1 teaspoon of dried) and leave to infuse in a jug or teapot for 5 minutes before drinking. Strain. Add a little honey or a slice of lemon if you like. Rosemary, sage and the various mints are particularly good; digestives include thyme, lime-flower and fennel (used to relieve colic in babies) and camomile to aid sleep.

Iced herb teas are refreshing during hot weather — try mint or lemon verbena. Make a large jug full, strain the herbs after 5 minutes and allow to cool. Serve with ice and a fresh sprig of the appropriate herb.

special note:

Anything that is to be stored for any length of time requires that the utmost care is taken in the cleanliness of its preparation. Ensure that all containers, spoons and stoppers are thoroughly sterilized.

scented sugars

WHEN MAKING CAKES and puddings, use scented sugars to subtly enhance the aroma and flavour of the recipe. Such aromatics include scented geranium leaves, scented rose petals, rosemary, lavender flower-heads, lemon verbena, mint, orange or lemon rind (allow the latter to dry in a warm place for a day before using). Ensure that the petals, leaves or herbs are dry, then simply fill a glass storage jar with the caster sugar, adding the aromatic items in layers. Leave in a warm room to infuse for a couple of weeks before use. Sieve the sugar before using. Vanilla pods (with the seeds scooped out as they would be for adding to desserts) can be used in the same way. Alternatively, you can grind up the vanilla pods in an electric grinder, mixing the fine grounds into the sugar for a really pungent aroma and flavour.

banishing unwanted smells

THE AROMA OF COOKING is the source of some of the most delicious smells in the house. However, not all cooking smells are good ones and the need to eliminate the bad and the lingering is made more acute since the kitchen, now more then ever before, is a place for socializing as much as for cooking. It may be wonderful to sit down to dinner surrounded by the fragrance of the boeuf bourguignonne that's been simmering in the oven for hours, but it's a different matter when the mackerel has caught fire under the grill.

Speed is of the essence, so quick fixes, such as burning a few sprigs of fresh rosemary, thyme or sage under the grill — or on the back of an Aga or range if you have one — to conquer the smell of less fragrant incinerations, are very useful. A generally fragrant ambience can be achieved if

RIGHT: *Nothing beats the smell of fresh garlic — raw or cooked. It's an exhilarating aroma, full of promise of the meal to come and a guarantee of delicious flavour when it does. Chew parsley to counteract garlic's lingering smell in the mouth.*

LEFT: *Burning a sprig or two of fresh rosemary on the hot plate of your range, or in a warm oven with the door left ajar, will disperse the lingering smell of burnt food and replace it with a sweet herbal aroma.*

you pop a few eucalyptus leaves into your oven as it cools down after cooking. Like juniper and thyme, eucalyptus has powerful antiseptic properties as its clean, astringent scent would suggest, so is a particularly suitable plant for kitchen use. If you can't get hold of the plants themselves, their essential oils are equally effective and, in fact, far more versatile. They can either be vaporized into the atmosphere using a conventional or electric burner, or they can be added to water for an instant spritz of sanitizing freshness. A quick room spray made up of a few drops of either eucalyptus, thyme, juniper, rosemary, lavender or lemon essential oil (according to preference for their - perfumes) is pleasant and effective.

Using culinary ingredients for fragrance or to overcome unwanted kitchen odours feels right in a way that blasting the atmosphere with commercially-fragranced sprays just doesn't, particularly in our increasingly polluted world. Extending the principles of a more natural, environmentally

vaporizing
mix for
de-odorizing
rooms

• 2 pods of vanilla

• 2-3 sticks of cinnamon

• 1 tablespoon cloves

Crush all ingredients into a
coarse mix in a mortar and
pestle. Slowly heat in a heavy
bottomed frying pan. When
the spices begin to smoke,
walk the pan through the
rooms that need freshening.
Re-heat as the pan cools down.

aware home — organic food, biodegradable washing powders, recycled rubbish — to the management of everyday smells seems to make sense. To remove smells in the fridge, try placing half a lemon with salt rubbed into its cut surface on a saucer. Replenish the salt until the lemon is dried out and then start the process again with another half. Another old-fashioned remedy for unwanted odours involves tipping coffee grounds down the plughole of a smelly sink and then slowly pouring a thin trickle of boiling water down after them. The grounds seem to absorb the nasty smells as they move through the system, and they won't block the drain. Used coffee grounds are also quite effective at combating smells in the fridge, and could be left there in a little bowl. For more general environmental smelliness, place saucers of milk (replenish daily) or a paste of mustard powder and water discreetly about the place — both absorb odours.

Boiling a few sprigs of rosemary, eucalyptus or thyme in a saucepan of water fills the air with their clean, outdoor scents. Or, if you do not have fresh herbs readily to hand, add a few drops of essential oils of lavender or thyme to a pan of boiling water. This method is particularly effective at overcoming the smell of stale cigarette and cigar smoke. Essential oils are, in fact, invaluable when it comes to overcoming unwanted household smells. If you can't immediately locate the source of a smell, combine a few drops of your favourite oil and some of benzoin, add half a teaspoon of scentless alcohol, such as vodka, for each drop of oil, place in a wide-brimmed bowl and allow the mixture to evaporate in the offending area. If you need to eliminate mustiness — say, in a guest room that has not been used for a while — choose clove or eucalyptus oil.

Masking odours with fragrance is effective, of course, but ironically, the thing that really seems to absorb unwanted smells is burning. This can easily be proved simply by lighting a match in a room where an unpleasant smell has developed — the odour seems to disappear into the flame. But this can be done in a much more fragrant way. The act of carrying around the kitchen a pan in

LEFT: *A smoking pan of warmed spices clears away unwanted odours. If the problem is widespread, you can walk around the house with the pan, wafting the aromas as you go.*

which cloves, cinnamon sticks and vanilla pods have been heated to smoking point is reminiscent of the ancient religious rituals that originally embraced and promoted the use of perfumes. The verb from which the word derives — *perfumare* — literally means 'through smoke'. Their spicy sweetness may not be an offering to propitiate the gods, but will fragrance the air with suspiciously dramatic speed.

The process of burning a scented substance — be it an incense stick, a piece of resinous frankincense or a compound of ground spices and dry herbs or berries — seems to eat up the tainted air. This practical effect informs the South American shamans' ancient practise of 'smudging', in which torches made from fragrant twigs are burned and the smoke carried from room to room as an act of purification and blessing.

one

two

Burning Incense

you will need

- 1 teaspoon cloves
- 1 teaspoon crushed aniseed
- 1 teaspoon bergamot
- 1 teaspoon crushed cinnamon
- 1 teaspoon crushed vanilla pod
- 2 teaspoons frankincense
- 2 teaspoons gum benzoin
- Essential oil
- 1 teaspoon sugar for a sweeter scent
- Pestle and mortar
- Screw-lidded jar

INCENSE STICKS ARE traditionally burned daily throughout houses in India and south-east Asia, a practise that defers to ancient spiritual cleansing rituals. Incense is widely available in a range of richly evocative aromas, and was chiefly burnt to dispel unwanted smells, made particularly acute by the climate. It is available in a range of lovely fragrances, but if you want to create your own fragrant mixture, you will need to invest in the necessary self-igniting charcoal discs on which to burn it. Lighting these takes patience — and several matches — but persevere, waiting for the crackling glow to develop into a slow smoulder. Place a tiny amount of whatever you choose to burn in the central depression of the disc and allow it to burn or melt gently. They are highly effective in absorbing odorous kitchen smells, musty rooms or even unpleasant animal odours. Keep the incense in a small lidded container, perhaps on a tray together with a small spoon handy. The discs will need to be kept in an airtight container to preserve their combustibility.

method

one Grind the spices and resins in the mortar and pestle (or electric grinder) as finely as you can. They should resemble a coarse powder. Add a few drops of the chosen essential oil and mix very thoroughly.

two Place into a container with a lid, such as a glass jar, and leave for at least a month in a cool dark cupboard. A quarter-teaspoonful of the mixture, placed onto the smoking charcoal disc, will be all you need to create an exotic pungent smell.

warning:

Make sure you've placed the disc on a heat-proof surface or in a solid heat-proof container, as it will get very, very hot as it burns • Take care not to burn yourself or allow the burning dish within a child's reach • The initial smoke does diffuse quickly to leave the fragrance lingering, but you'd be well advised to disconnect any smoke alarms while incense is burning • Never leave a burning disc unattended.

household cleaning

window
cleaner

*Vinegar leaves windows
shining*

• 1 part white distilled
  vinegar

• juice of 1 lemon

• 3 parts hot water.

Either mix together into a
bucket or a spray bottle. Rub
down with a scrim cloth or
crumpled newspaper. Works well
on tiles, too. In the summer
months, wipe down with a
damp cloth impregnated with
fly-repelling essential oils —
try lavender, lemongrass or
citronella. Make up a quick
solution of 10 drops of oil to
50 ml (2 fl oz) water. Shake
well before spraying onto
the cloth.

AS OUR AWARENESS GROWS OF the harm done to the environment by even the most everyday of chemicals, alternative household cleaning methods become more and more appealing. Employing techniques and natural products that have stood the test of time has a further advantage: that of avoiding the intrusion of synthetically scented products and harsh smelling chemicals into an otherwise naturally scented home. Replacing your battery of kitchen surface cleaners, oven cleaners, anti-bacterial sprays and polishes may sound radical and impractical, but in fact you need very little in the way of alternative products and equipment to achieve a great deal. Simply investing in white distilled vinegar, bicarbonate of soda, borax, washing soda and a few plastic spray bottles will give you all you need for revolutionary, effective natural cleaning.

Vinegar is invaluable for cleaning fridges (wipe away carefully afterwards to avoid residual fumes) or, mixed with an equal quantity of water, to descale kettles and make windows and ceramic tiles gleam. A cupful of vinegar in a bucket of warm water makes light work of cleaning wooden floors. Bicarbonate of soda, mixed with water to form a hard-working paste or sprayable solution, is a general all-purpose cleaner, scourer, polish and fungicide. Use a paste to clean your oven: leave it on to work for an hour and then rinse clean. When mixed in equal quantities with borax, bicarbonate of soda can also be used as dishwashing powder.

Borax is a brilliant stain-remover and disinfectant — soak clothes in a solution of 1 part borax to 8 parts water. It also makes an alternative oven cleaner when mixed with washing-up liquid. Washing soda clears blocked drains and a tablespoonful dissolved in a pan of hot water with a couple of aluminium milk bottle tops cleans silver flatware brilliantly. Everyday salt can be used as a mildly disinfectant scouring powder; mixed with lemon juice it can clean copper pans and remove rust stains. Lemon juice or vinegar mixed with olive oil cleans and polishes furniture, but a good old-fashioned beeswax polish is hard to beat (see page 42).

LEFT: *Using natural products like borax, bicarbonate of soda and vinegar to clean the home makes good sense if you are seeking to preserve a level of natural fragrance. Antiseptic and anti-bacterial essential oils can be added for fragrance and extra efficacy.*

Essential oils can improve the drudgery of household chores with both their fragrance and their powerful antiseptic, anti-bacterial properties. Added to a spray of bicarbonate of soda and water, the oils will compound the mixture's cleaning effect. Simply adding a drop or two of eucalyptus, lavender, lemon, pine, thyme, juniper or rosemary to a damp cloth for wiping down your surfaces turns the action into a pleasure. Be inventive: fragrant oils can be used wherever and whenever a surge of scent might transform a domestic task.

one   two   three

Lavender beeswax furniture polish

you will need

- 225 g (8 oz) pure unrefined beeswax
- 25 g (1 oz) soap flakes
- 570 ml (1 pint) genuine turpentine
- 570ml (1 pint) water
- 20 drops of lavender essential oil (or cedarwood or rosemary)
- Bain-marie
- Measuring jug
- Saucepan
- Scales
- Wooden spatula/spoon
- Sealable tin or jar to store finished polish

THIS BASIC RECIPE has been used for generations. It is simple, natural and has the distinctive smell of beeswax and turpentine. Add a little lavender essential oil to enhance the smell and act as an insecticide. Apply a small amount to the surface of your furniture, polishing with a soft cloth. It will nourish the wood and provide a healthy sheen, while the subtle aromatics of lavender will also deter insects from settling on the surface — a bonus during the summer months when flies can be a irritating menace.

The recipe for a simple floor wax derives from the same principles and is perfect for feeding and shining terracotta and brick as well as wood floors. Made from unrefined beeswax and turpentine, mixed in a ratio of 225 g (8 oz) to 850 ml ($1\frac{1}{2}$ pints), the two are heated together to blend.

method

one Make sure you have all the ingredients and equipment you need to hand before you begin.

two Slowly melt the beeswax with the turpentine in the top of the bain-marie. This process must be done gently over a simmering heat, as turpentine is highly inflammable. As soon as the beeswax has melted, remove from the heat and allow to cool. Now put the water into a saucepan and bring to the boil. Add the soap flakes, slowly stirring until melted, then allow to cool.

three Slowly pour the cooled (still warm) liquid soap mixture into the soft beeswax mixture. It should make a thick creamy consistency. Now add the drops of essential oils, mixing in thoroughly. Finally, pour into a lidded container.

keeping invaders at bay

**t w i g g y
f l y   d e t e r r e n t**

Add drops of essential oil onto strips of fabric or ribbon that are artfully tied to a decorative bunch of dried stems. Position it strategically in the centre of the room where flies commonly gather, or by a window or doorway to repel their entry. Use basil, citronella, geranium, lavender, lemongrass, rosemary, thyme, peppermint (particularly for mosquitoes) and patchouli.

JUST AS KITCHENS are magnets to sociable people, they are also — less happily — irresistible to insects and rodents. Your armoury of fragrant herbs and essential oils comes into its own yet again in this department, obviating the need for toxic sprays and inhumane poisons. If you can create an environment that is unappealing to insects in the first instance, you avoid the need to kill them.

Many plants have their own defence systems when it comes to insects, so harnessing them for our use seems a natural step. The medieval practise of strewing herbs through the rushes on the floor was a deliberate method of deterring 'flies, vermin and foul airs', tansy (*Tanacetum vulgare*) being the most popular and effective. We would baulk at deliberately strewing anything on our floors these days, but you might like to place dried bunches of tansy, lavender or rosemary — or a mixture — on the floor of food cupboards or the larder. A level of ambient fragrance that irritates our flying visitors is a good start, so try hanging bunches of herbs in vulnerable areas. Many pelargoniums are blessed with highly scented leaves which insects dislike, so growing these on or beneath kitchen window-sills or in pots inside can have a positive effect. Peppermint is famously unpleasant to mice, so if you do have a problem, try scattering leaves around the boundaries of any affected area and at the entrance of holes. Raw onions studded with cloves and suspended on string help to deter flies and bring a homely scent to a kitchen or larder. Another ruse, using the same ingredients, is to boil a few onions studded with one or two cloves until they are soft, cut them into slices and leave these on saucers hidden about the place; change the onions for fresh ones every two or three days.

LEFT: *Lengths of coloured cotton ribbon can be impregnated with the anti-insect oil of your choice, tied to a dried bunch of fine twigs and suspended from the ceiling of a room where needed.*

Keeping herbs that have insecticidal properties at strategic points around the kitchen will deter unwanted invaders. Tansy has been used against insect pests since the Middle Ages, and its attractive foliage, combined here with primulas and parsley, makes a simple, good-looking arrangement.

onion and clove pomanders

The subtle smell of onions and cloves will help repel flies in the kitchen. Cut an onion in half horizontally and cut away most of the skin. Using a sharp knife, carefully cut 1 cm (³/₈ in) in around the cut edge. Stud whole cloves along this line. Knot one end of a piece of string and thread from the cut side up through the middle of the onion, using a heavy-duty needle.

RIGHT: *The unattractiveness to flies of the smell of onions and cloves has been put to good use in the kitchen for years. Suspend halves of onions studded with cloves in any areas where flies are a problem.*

The insecticide power of many essential oils can be used in a number of ways. Citronella is the most commonly used — commercially available garden candles are frequently scented with it — and can be applied to strips of cotton or ribbon that are then tied near windows and doors. Make up a room spray of around 5-10 drops in 50 ml (2 fl oz) of water for a quick fumigation, or apply drops of neat oil to window-sills and the inside edges of curtains or blinds. Cotton wool balls with the oil dropped on them can be left in saucers at strategic points, and of course the usual methods of vaporizing oils can be used inside and out — a burner beneath the table is perfect when you're sitting out for a summer's evening and would rather enjoy yourselves without attendant mosquitoes. If the powerful fragrance of citronella isn't your thing, then look at geranium, eucalyptus, peppermint, bergamot, juniper, lavender, clove, rosemary or patchouli, which are all fragrant insecticides.

insecticides

Here are some ideas for killing unwanted flies in the kitchen area, avoiding the use of chemically-based fly sprays. Hang bunches of insect-repelling herbs, or position arrangements in a vase on a window-sill or near an open door to help to deter some flies. Tansy, rue, pennyroyal, rosemary or southernwood, as well as lavender, are all considered effective.

The Spanish traditionally use sticky roots of elecampane as a natural fly trap, hanging them from open windows to attract and catch the flies.

Make up a sweet-smelling natural fly spray for immediate use by blending 10 drops of citronella and lavender essential oils diluted in 50 ml (2 fl oz) of purified water. Shake vigorously. Alternatively, try one of the following: geranium, lavender, lemongrass, rosemary, thyme, peppermint, patchouli.

Attract flies to a sweet-smelling saucer of sticky treacle. Alternatively, boil 50 g (2 oz) of quassia chipped bark with 570 ml (1 pint) of water. Simmer for 20 minutes. Add 50 g (2 oz) sugar. Cool. Place in bowls in strategic positions near an open window.

CHAPTER 3

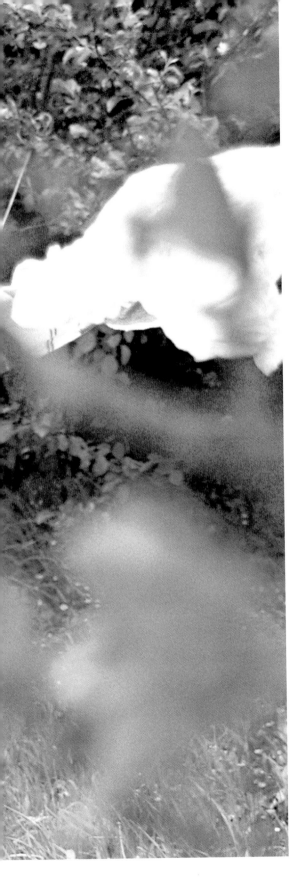

THE LAUNDRY

WASHING AND IRONING are perhaps two of our least favourite household obligations, yet since there's no avoiding them, the more enjoyable we can make them the better. The challenge of turning these chores into pleasures is ably — and seriously — met by fragrance. If the acts of washing, drying, pressing and storing your clothes are enhanced by scent, then the battle of persuading ourselves to undertake them is all but won.

washing

THE IDEAL IS TO EMULATE the old-fashioned country tradition of clothing dried in the fresh air, either on washing lines held aloft by wooden poles or spread out in the sun over lavender or rosemary bushes — or simply on the grass, as described in Beatrix Potter's paeon to perfect laundry, *The Tale of Mrs Tiggy Winkle*. Very few of us these days have the opportunity to undertake such practises literally, though if you can, there's really nothing to beat the crisp freshness of clothes dried in the open air. Otherwise, fragrance can bring the sensory experience closer. For a lingering, warp-and-weft-deep scent, try adding herbal waters to the final rinse of hand-washed clothing — a particular treat for precious garments or delicate baby clothes.

LEFT: *Drying clothes outside gives them a uniquely fresh fragrance. If you have lavender or rosemary bushes, try draping small items of clothing over them to dry, so the scent of the flowers is absorbed into the fabric.*

Create the illusion of outdoor drying by making your own tumble-dryer smell heavenly. A few drops of rosemary oil, or whichever essential oil you prefer, on a scrap of fabric can be popped into your dryer and the whole laundry load will emerge with that unmistakable breezy fragrance.

Buy large bottles of rose water and add a generous splash when rinsing delicate hand-washed clothes. It is usually cost effective to buy rose water from ethnic food stores and supermarkets where it is often sold in 1 litre (1½ pint) bottles.

To make a simple herbal infusion, simply add a generous bunch of fresh herbs to a pan of boiling water. Try rosemary, lavender, lemon balm, mint or sweet marjoram and bay. These are all herbs that grow quite prolifically during the summer months. Use whatever you have an abundance of and like the smell of. Otherwise use dried — approximately 25 g (1oz) to 1½ litres (3 pints) of water. Leave to steep in the boiling water with a lid on for 5-10 minutes. Strain through a fine sieve (or muslin) and add to your final rinse.

household soap

A useful soap with antiseptic and stain-removing properties.

200 g (8 oz) soap flakes
20 ml (1 fl oz) olive oil
100 ml (3½ fl oz) water
1 teaspoon eucalyptus essential oil
1 teaspoon tea tree essential oil

Slowly melt the soap flakes with the olive oil in a bain-marie, stirring with a wooden spoon. When melted, transfer to a clean saucepan and add the oils, mixing well. Continue until the mixture has formed a stiff paste. Transfer to an oiled mould — any household container will do.

Aromatic Lavender Ironing Water

one

two

three

you will need

- 300 ml (10 fl oz) purified water
- 25 ml (1 fl oz) vodka, 90% proof
- 15 drops lavender essential oil — or rosemary, geranium or rose
- Measuring jug
- 2 screw top bottles
- Spray bottle

THERE IS SOMETHING wonderfully uplifting and comforting in the scent of recently ironed linen and cotton, so the addition of a favourite fragrance to that evocative mix is undoubtedly a winner. Nothing seems more appropriate to an ironing room than the scent of lavender, associated for centuries with the virtues of good household management and cleanliness. Lavender is powerfully anti-bacterial (able to destroy the typhoid bacilli, diptheria, pneumococcus and streptococcus) and a natural insecticide. It is also noted for its calming effect, which might go some way to making ironing a reasonably pleasurable task!

one Add the oil to the vodka in a sterilized bottle.

two Swirl to mix and leave for 24 hours. Measure out the purified water in a sterilized jug and add. Decant into a sterilized screw top bottle.

three When ready for use, pour into a spray bottle and mist your laundry as you iron for a lovely, refreshing scent.

warning: *Make sure that you don't put essential oils directly into your iron, as they may leave deposits.*

ironing

FRAGRANCED IRONING WATERS seem to be *de rigeur* if we are to believe everything we read, as more and more exclusive fragrance houses bring out their own versions. Their sudden popularity is understandable. The simple addition of lavender essential oil to your spray bottle of water allows its wonderfully fresh scent to fill the air every time you use it as you iron. Experiment with other oils — lemon, rosemary, geranium or rose, for example. Refresh the bottle each time you iron as the oils do begin to lose their potency.

Fragranced ironing waters, however fashionable and widely available, are never going to make ironing anything less than the hard work it is. But fragrance can certainly enhance the process. In addition, you can ensure that you are combining scent with hygiene by using the trusted anti-bacterial oils — lavender as mentioned, but also rosemary, lemon and pine. This is particularly relevant now that very few of us ever use the germ-killing boil-wash cycle.

storing

TAKING PRIDE AND PLEASURE in your laundry implies equal care in storing it. Your beautifully fragrant, carefully ironed clothing, bedding and towels deserve to be kept well ordered and sweet smelling. One of the most familiar and traditional methods of bringing fragrance to specific areas for specific purposes is to make scented bags or sachets. Slipped into drawers, between sheets in airing cupboards, inside shoes and into storage chests, these can contain almost limitless combinations of dried fragrant ingredients.

The very act of making scented bags is a pleasure — handling the raw ingredients, sifting them between your fingers, sewing all those sensual treats inside a beautiful fabric parcel. The very simplest and most traditional is, of course, the humble lavender bag. Humble, even

lemon soap ball

An old Tudor recipe, which is extremely effective in removing any organic stains on fabric. Simply rub onto the stain and either put the article to soak in cold water or wash in the normal way.

- 100 g (4 oz) grated olive oil soap or pure soap flakes
- 2 small lemons
- 1 heaped teaspoon alum (available from pharmacies)

Chop up the lemons into very small pieces, removing the pips. Place in a mortar and pestle with the soap flakes and alum. Pound vigorously until you have a stiff paste. Mould it into a ball and place onto some kitchen paper. Place in the airing cupboard to dry and harden for a week before use.

predictable it may be, but lavender is still one of the most versatile and popular of all flowers. Used alone, its clean powdery fragrance carries with it all the nostalgia of pristine household management as it used to be. Simple muslin bags filled with dried lavender and tied with knotted ribbons are unbeatable purveyors of its uniquely cleansing scent, easily refreshed as the flowers' fragrance recedes with new lavender or a few drops of essential oil.

There's no need to limit yourself to this ultimate retro fragrance, though adopting the concept of 'layering' fragrance from the world of perfumery is a lovely way to reinforce the scent of your laundry. The simpler the method you choose to adopt the better: a lavender rinse, followed by a lavender tumble-dry, followed by a lavender-scented pressing, followed by storage amidst lavender, for instance, is effortless, but has delicious results.

In addition to their fragrancing role, scented bags can be adapted to serve particular purposes. If you need to de-odorize shoes for day-to-day wear, for example, or keep destructive moths at bay without resorting to those eye-watering, camphor-based balls sold commercially for the purpose, it's simply a matter of filling bags with the relevant dry ingredients or essential oils. Interlace stored clothes with little bags filled with a mixture of cinnamon, cloves, black pepper, southernwood and orris root, ground in a pestle and mortar — deliciously spicy and effective against moths. Cedarwood has long been respected as an efficient deterrent to most insects. In Imperial China, strips of its bark were placed between layers of stored laundry. The ultimate storage chests are made of cedar or camphor, both woods lending the stored contents a subtle and unforgettably exotic flavour and protecting them from invading insects. Few of us, however, can run to such luxuries, but cedar hangers or cedar balls and leaves that can be popped into drawers and chests make good fragrant compromises.

Other traditional ideas for keeping unwanted pests from enjoying your clothes while you're not wearing them, include putting fresh geranium leaves (preferably between two pieces of kitchen roll) in among folded garments, or adding a few drops of cedar or rosemary oil to cotton wool balls and enclosing them in a pillowcase, which can then be laid among your clothes. Those lucky enough to have a walnut tree growing in their garden might like to know that moths hate the smell of walnut leaves, which can be used in much the same way as the geranium leaves.

The pleasure of opening a drawer to a rush of subtle fragrance is second only to that of enjoying the smell of your clothes once they are on your body. An effective trick that also makes a lovely present is perfumed drawer lining paper. Choose any kind of paper, cut it to size and roll the sheets together. Then seal the roll in a plastic bag with a sheet of blotting paper on which you have dropped your essential oil combinations. Leave it for about a week to allow the perfume to permeate the papers. These can also be customized with anti-insect oils.

LEFT: Grow scented geraniums and pelargoniums for fragrance and colour — and as a useful supply of natural insecticide. Pots placed on window-sills will keep flies at bay, and the leaves can protect clothes from moths.

Aromatic Bags & Sachets

you will need

Equal amounts of:

• cloves

• cinnamon

• southernwood

• black pepper

• orris root

• Finely woven linen or

  cotton fabric

• Mortar and pestle

• Weighing scales

• Pinking shears

• Sewing kit

KEEP MOTHS AT BAY without resorting to moth balls with a deliciously aromatic mixture of cinnamon, cloves, black pepper, southernwood and orris root ground in a pestle and mortar and slipped into little muslin bags. To make something special of your moth bags, run up small drawstring bags using delicate fabrics such as this translucent gold organza to contain the basic moth bag. If you are making them to give away as gifts, photocopy a print of a moth and slip it inside the bag, so its role to the recipient is instantly identifiable. Or you could even decide to embroider a moth onto the bag, or choose a fabric that incorporates a pattern of moths and butterflies.

An alternative idea to the one described below is to create little sachets containing a mixture of freshly dried herbs. These bags will have a lighter perfume — perhaps suitable for storing summer clothes, reserving the heavier aromatic mix for a winter wardrobe. Try mixing 3 parts lavender with 3 parts lemon verbena, 3 parts scented geranium leaves and 1 part rosemary. Grind them together in a pestle and mortar or with an electric grinder, and fill the bags as outlined below.

method

one Assemble the ingredients: from the left, black pepper, cinnamon, cloves, southernwood and orris root.

two Grind each ingredient coarsely either in a mortar and pestle or an electric grinder. Mix together in a bowl.

three Cut out a small oblong of finely woven fabric, such as linen or cotton. Any spare scraps will do. Use pinking shears to help prevent fraying around the edges. Fold in half and sew together along two sides, leaving the third side open. Make up a wide-ended funnel by wrapping a sheet of paper into a cone and securing with a piece of adhesive tape. Use to pour mixed spices into the bag — enough to fill it loosely. Pin and sew final side together.

Either slip the finished, filled bag amongst your folded clothes — particularly clothes that are stored away for the season — hang from a coat hanger.

three

RIGHT: *Look out for unusual fabrics in delicate loose weaves from which to make lavender bags. Trim the edges with a few beads or ribbons for a finishing touch.*

decorative lavender bags

FILLED WITH THE SEASONS new crop of lavender, a single large bag will scent an entire cupboard or wardrobe. Hidden amongst linen in an airing cupboard, a bag takes on even greater pungency. Instead of the more predictable muslin or cottons, look out for remnants of more exotic embroidered fabrics, such as this silvery organza, for a touch of feminine luxury. Decorated around the edges with tiny silver beads, this bag would make a gorgeous gift. Cut fabric to approximately 30 x 50 cm (12 x 20 in). Fill with plain lavender flowers, adding a small scrap of fabric roughly the same colour as the lavender, impregnated with a few drops of lavender essential oil to heighten the effect of the flowers. Experiment with mixtures of lavender and other ingredients. Try cardamom (crush the pods, or just use the seeds), sweet marjoram, rosemary, lemon verbena, rose, scented geranium leaves, thyme, spearmint, peppermint, applemint and eau de cologne mint.

LEFT: *Keep shoes fresh by stuffing them with pretty de-odorizing bags filled with a mixture of dried lavender, sage, peppermint and eucalyptus leaves.*

shoe bags

FILL LONG, THIN LINEN bags with a mix of de-odorizing lavender, sage, peppermint and eucalyptus to revive shoes. Place them inside overnight so that the shoes smell fresh and sweet the next day.

herbs for strewing

PUT HERBS INTO SACHETS or strew them between two layers of cotton organza or tissue paper. Or simply tie bouquets to lay onto linen or to string up from one of the shelves in an airing cupboard. Any of the following herbs can be used, either alone or mixed in various combinations: lavender, southernwood, wormwood, santolina, rosemary, sweet woodruff, spearmint, peppermint and rue (although the leaves can cause skin irritations) All these herbs repel insects. Experiment with varying combinations to create your own personal recipe.

- Wooden coat hanger with screw-in metal hook. Piece of cotton wadding (polyester will do) slightly longer than the coat hanger — enough to comfortably wrap around both sides Piece of fabric the length of the coat hanger plus 4 cm (1$^1\!/_2$ in) times the width of the coat hanger, plus an extra 4 cm (1$^1\!/_2$ in)
- Sewing machine
- Needle, thread and tacking thread
- Pins
- Scissors
- 15 g (about $^1\!/_2$ oz) fresh dried lavender per hanger.
- Optional extra: approx. 30 cm (12 in) length of fine matching ribbon.

Scented Coat Hangers

A LOVELY WAY TO LOCK FRAGRANCE inside clothes and cupboards is by using scented coat hangers. Their fragrance lingers in the fabric of whatever garment is hung on them, and a small length of beautiful fabric and some dried lavender are all you need to transform an ordinary wooden coat hanger into something pretty and distinctively pungent. Hangers are perennially popular gifts and are easy to make; and only three or four will fill a wardrobe with scent. Variations could include adding dried rosemary or lemon verbena; or try spicing the lavender up with just a little crushed cloves, cinnamon bark (roughly ground up in mortar and pestle) or cardamom pods. When the scent begins to fade add a couple of drops of lavender essential oil to the coat hanger (in a discreet place alongside a seam to avoid any fabric discolouring).

one   two   three

method

one Cut the wadding to size. Fold in half and find the centre point. Snip a hole in the wadding, and pass the coat hanger hook over it. Lie flat on a table, folding the wadding over the coat hanger. (Do not unscrew hook yet, as once the hole is covered with wadding and a layer of fabric, it will be difficult to find it again.)

two Take a needle and length of tacking thread. Start to sew one end section of the wadding together, using a simple over stitch. Then sprinkle a generous amount of lavender on both sides of the coat hanger, working a small section at a time, then sewing it up. When you reach the other end, stitch the wadding firmly together to enclose the hanger.

three Measure the decorative fabric along the length and width. With right sides together, fold in half length ways and either hand stitch or machine stitch along one end and along the length. Invert and press. Now slide onto the hanger. When you reach the hook, unscrew, pass over the hole to the end (you should feel the hole in the wadding). Make a hole in the fabric with a sharp instrument (such as a fine knitting needle) and screw the hook back in. Finally, sew up the end with matching thread. Finish with a length of narrow ribbon tied in a bow around the hook, if you wish.

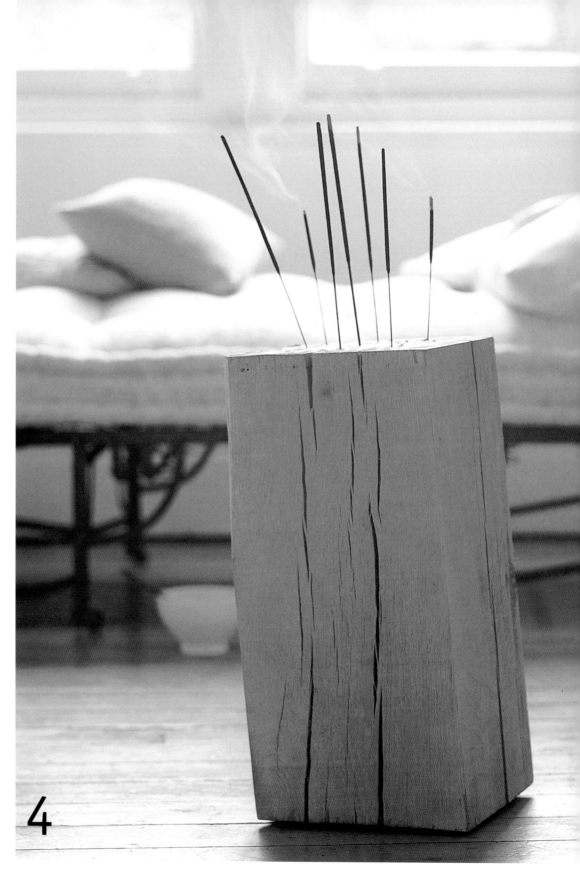

CHAPTER 4

THE SCENTED ROOM

EVERY HOUSE HAS its own family of scents that unite to give it individuality — organic, artificial, material and personal. The smells create a revealing aromatic picture that unfolds as we pass from room to room. Like a picture, the sensory image produced becomes instantly recognizable, even if only on a subconscious level: we're never quite sure why we feel so at home or why a place feels so uncannily familiar. Layers of additional fragrance are a matter of personal taste and, like clothing, can be changed to suit the season or the mood.

fresh flowers

AS WITH SO MUCH IN LIFE, simplicity is often the best rule to apply when it comes to perfuming the home, and it goes without saying that the simplest and most natural way to fill a room with fragrance is to bring in fresh flowers. The choice is huge, both from the garden and from the florist. Decadent, waxy lilies, with their emphatic, glistening stamens and staining pollen, have a perfume that almost makes you dizzy; blowsy, petal-dropping roses picked from a summer garden have a subtle scent; and a jasmine plant studded with star-like flowers or a gloriously heady hyacinth have a powerful fragrance that can fill a room instantaneously. Sweet peas pack a surprising aromatic punch for their size and appearance; and delicate mimosa, with all its warm associations with southern France, is covered in tiny yellow, ball-like flowers that exude a peppery, honeyed sweetness. You can compound the effect by opening windows whenever the weather allows, so that the smells from gardens, trees or nearby parks — plus the inevitable and welcome rush of fresh air — combines with those you have introduced inside. The life-affirming scent of freshly mown summer grass travels quite a distance and should be enjoyed as often as possible.

After the privations of a northern winter, nothing refreshes the senses more delightfully than the arrival in our gardens, hedgerows and parks of spring flowers. Their optimistic assaults on frosty ground gladden the heart with the promise of warmer days to come. Brilliant hues of acid yellow, gold, coral, cobalt, indigo and pink suddenly invade our lives and should also be encouraged to invade our homes, bringing with them their strong, invigorating perfumes.

OPPOSITE: *Instant spring for your home in the shape of sculptural blue hyacinths. With their intensely fragrant flowers, they make a dramatic statement in contemporary glass containers.*

BELOW: *The delicacy of many flowers belies the force of their fragrance. The scent of jasmine is at the heart of many of the world's finest perfumes.*

'Roseraie de l'Hay', one
of the most beautiful and
intensely scented of the
rugosa roses, flowers all
summer long.

The undisputed king of spring fragrance is the hyacinth. Its perfume is fantastically sweet and pervasive. Planted in terracotta pots, moss-filled baskets or zinc buckets, groups of hyacinths in pink, white or every shade of indigo are one of the easiest, prettiest room fragrancers of all. They are wonderful as cut flowers, too, but remember not to sever the base of their bulbous, sap-filled white stems if you really want them to last.

Flowers picked straight from the garden somehow hold their scent in a way that forced, shop flowers just don't. This is particularly true of roses, so if you have a garden, make the most of it by planting old-fashioned varieties that carry the truest, richest perfumes. Choose Bourbon, Damask, Gallica and Rugosa species for their intense fragrance and fantastic palette of petal colours. A generous bowl of heavy-headed roses with petals in every shade of magenta, crimson and pink, some frilled, some speckled or striated, makes a mouthwatering focal point in any room and will fill the atmosphere with fragrance. As the petals drop and dry, save them for use in pot pourri recipes, recycling your enjoyment of both their colour and scent throughout the year.

Add a little bicarbonate of soda and salt to the water to keep flowers fresh as long as possible. Cut a small piece of stem off every day. Hard, woody stems should be split a couple of centimetres (just under an inch) from the bottom. When giving flowers as a gift, wrap them in several sheets of damp paper and a final wrap of water-resistant cellophane. Dip the stems into melted wax. Add a reminder note to the recipient to cut off the base of the stems before plunging them into cold water.

Bringing fruits as well as flowers into the home extends its aromatic range. A bowl of fruit left to ripen in a room will lightly scent the air — apples, oranges and autumnal quinces having particularly delicious fragrance. The rural tradition of hanging fresh hops around doorways and fireplaces to dry is one to revive at home to enjoy the soothing mellow scent of the drying heads.

ABOVE: *Bringing flowers and herbs into the home is a delightful way to enjoy the benefits of nature. Hops make beautiful decorative additions to doorways and mantelpieces and give out a gentle and soothing fragrance.*

Lavender bushes, whether in the garden or on window-sills, afford us visual as well as aromatic pleasure. Their indigo flowerheads create a mist of summer colour and, once dried, retain their unmistakable fragrance — sweet, warm and piercing — better than almost any other plant. The wonder of this smell explains the ubiquity of lavender in every aspect of perfumery. Maximize on lavender's versatility by popping a sprig or two inside your hoover bag for a waft of fragrance as you vacuum, or freshen a guest bedroom in the traditional way by scattering dried lavender heads (or a mixture of lavender and the damp tea-leaves so beloved by Mrs Beeton for their dust-laying properties) over the carpet and sweeping them to the skirtings to be left as a fragrant border. The action of brushing itself compresses the flowers and releases the pungence of their oil. Flies hate the smell of lavender, so a sprinkling of lavender oil around the window frame or on the curtain linings can keep them at bay. A more decorative method would be to create garlands of flowers to hang by open windows, or in the bathroom or cloakroom.

BELOW: Make a simple hanging lavender pomander by covering a heart-shaped base of oasis with lavender flowerheads, stuck on with PVA glue.

lavender pomander

A SCENTED TOKEN for a loved one comes in no better form than a lavender pomander. If you are lucky enough to receive one, hang it by your desk light to create a fragrant zone while you work.

Using a kitchen knife, shape a piece of oasis into a heart, or perhaps into the first letter of a name. First, slice the oasis the thickness you require, and then draw your design before carefully cutting it out. Smear the surface with PVA glue and then sprinkle it with dried lavender, coating it generously and pressing down firmly to make sure the lavender adheres. When the glue has dried, do the same on the reverse side and on the narrow edge sides. Apply glue with a paintbrush to touch up any gaps and fill these with more lavender.

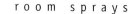

YOUR COLLECTION of essential oils can be used wherever and whenever you like to emulate the glorious fragrance of fresh flowers, fruit and herbs. Used as a room spray or vaporized from a burner, electric vaporizer or light-bulb ring, oils can refresh, soothe, stimulate and comfort as they fill the air with scent. Much research

de-odorizing room spray

Place the following essential oils in a sterilized bottle and leave for 24 hours: 80 drops bergamot, 60 drops lavender, 30 drops lemon. Add 25 ml (1 fl oz) 90% proof vodka , mix well and leave for another 48 hours. Add 25 ml (1 fl oz) of distilled water and blend. Pour into a sterilized 50 ml (2 fl oz) atomizer bottle, and keep in a cool dark cupboard.

has been done to establish the various therapeutic effects of oils, and it is interesting to observe their growing application in industrial and office environments, too. Some Japanese companies are deliberately pumping aromas around their buildings, tailored to specific effects: lavender and rose to soothe the spirit in public areas; lemon to increase alertness in precision work areas, and so on. Another key environmental service offered by essential oils is to combat the debilitating effects of air-borne pollutants from computers, air-conditioning, cigarette smoke and chemicals. While related problems are never as acute at home as they are at work, it is still worth considering the impact of such pollution in your domestic environment. In tandem with ionizers, which rebalance the negative and positive ions in the air and can dramatically improve unhealthy atmospheres, vaporizing or spraying oils with particularly strong anti-bacterial properties — such as lavender, petitgrain, lemon, rosemary, sandalwood, juniper, patchouli, tea tree or cedar — around affected rooms will have a noticeably beneficial effect on the quality of the air. After a particularly smoky party or dinner, a quick morning-after fumigation can be achieved by putting a few drops of thyme or lavender essential oils in a saucepan of water and leaving it to simmer for as long as you can.

pot pourri

AMID THE PANOPLY of home-fragrancing methods, pot pourri has long been a favourite. At its best, it combines the colours and forms of its component flowers, barks and spices with their subtle scents and is a natural, decorative way to distribute perfume throughout the house. It tends to be associated in our minds, as are orange and clove pomanders, with the rather less than fragrant sixteenth century, when its odour-eating power was positively vital for civilized living. Pot pourri's longevity speaks volumes for its effectiveness and for its simplicity. The snobbery that has arisen in recent years against its use is probably a result of the distinctly inferior stuff that is so cheaply and widely available. This pale imitation is based largely on commercially fragranced and hectically dyed

OPPOSITE: Room sprays are wonderfully effective ways of freshening and scenting the atmosphere, so keep bottles to hand around the house for use as required.

LEFT: Make a feature of fragrance by displaying pot pourri in a stunning, organically-shaped wooden bowl. Silica-dried peony heads have been used to add colour and beauty to the scented mixture.

ABOVE: *The beauty of pot pourri is as much in the forms and colours of its ingredients as it is in the delicacy of its scent.*

RIGHT: *Display your pot pourri in beautiful and unusual containers. This old metal cup allows the positioning of little pockets of fragrance on side tables or mantelpieces without compromising on space.*

wood shavings. But once you've experienced the real thing, you'll want to use it everywhere.

Traditionally, pot pourri was based on the eternally fragrant rose, the luscious colours of the heaped fading petals brightening the rooms they scented. Other fragrant ingredients have increasingly made their mark: jasmine, peony, carnation pinks, scented geraniums and lavender, combined with dried herbs and roughly ground spices such as cinnamon, cloves and star anise — even chips of fragrant sandalwood or cedar, pine needles and dried citrus peel. The combinations are limitless, but the simpler the better. Essential oils are useful in prolonging the fragrance of any mixture, a few drops of the relevant oil being scattered over the pot pourri as the scent begins to recede. Choose how you display your pot pourri with care and imagination. An enclosed container will prolong the life of the fragrance, but open bowls allow you to enjoy the sight as well as the smell. Antique dishes or large wooden bowls make perfect recepticles for side tables and mantelpieces, but you might like to have a wide bowl of pot pourri on your coffee table or hall console that your guests can run their fingers through to enjoy and to disperse the scent. Add silica-dried flower heads in beautiful colours to enhance the dish. Alternatively, you might like to make little bags or sachets for your pot pourri to carry the fragrance wherever you choose.

M a k i n g   P o t   P o u r r i

A rich, spicy mix, redolent of

winter festivities.

you will need

• 600 g (1¼ lb) semi-dried

  rose petals

• 25g (1oz) eucalyptus, bay

  and fresh pine leaves.

• 225 g (8 oz) coarse sea salt

• 25 g (1oz) dried orange peel

• 25 g (1oz) powdered orris root

• 25 g (1oz) powder gum benzoin

• 25 g (1 oz) crushed

  cinnamon sticks

• 25 g (1oz) crushed coriander

  seeds

• 15g (¾ oz) cloves

• 10g (¼ oz) ground nutmeg

Essential oils:

• 50 drops orange

• 30 drops frankincense

• 30 drops bergamot

• 30 drops cedarwood

• 20 drops cinnamon

• 20 drops clove

• 20 drops myrrh

POT POURRI IS ONE of the most traditional and possibly one of the most effective ways of scenting a room. Properly made, the mix of flowers, spices and oils is most enduring.

There are two ways of making pot pourri, one created using what is known as the moist method, the other using the so-called dry method. The former involves a more lengthy process and the resultant pot pourri requires time to mature. However, it is time well spent, as the finished product generally lasts for many years.

To ensure that the short-lived scents of many of the ingredients used in pot pourris and herbal sachets retain their aromas for a reasonable period of time, a fixative must be used. Orris root, which is from the rhizome *Iris fiorentina,* is often used. It is cheap, easily available and, smelling faintly of violets, has the ability to maximize the power of other scents. Gum benzoin is another strong fixative. It is derived from the styrax benzoin tree and has a sweet, balsamic vanilla scent. These two recipes are from Angela Flanders, who is well known in the industry for creating the ultimate pot pourri.

moist method

one Place a layer about 1 cm (½ in) thick of the dried flower and herb mix at the bottom of a straight-sided container with a lid. Cut out a cardboard disc to fit the inside of the jar and weigh it down until the mix is uniformly compressed. Cover with a layer of salt. Continue in layers until the jar is full, ending with a layer of salt. If you have not filled the jar, you can always add to it as more flowers become available, as long as you always finish with a layer of salt. Leave for approximately 6-8 weeks for the mixture to mature.

two Remove the dried flower and herb mix from the jar and break it up into a crumbly consistency. Now mix up the spices, fixatives and essential oils in a separate bowl. Add these to the pot pourri mix in a large bowl, stirring with a wooden spoon. When well mixed, transfer the pot pourri back into the original container, pressing it down firmly. Leave to mature for at least 2 months — the longer you can resist using it the better.

dry pot pourri

A reinvention of the traditional
English rose-based favourite.

you will need

- 225 g (8 oz) dried rose
  heads, petals, buds
- 175 g (6 oz) lavender flowers
- 50 g (2 oz) rose leaves
- 25 g (1 oz) orris root powder
- 15 g (³⁄₄ oz) gum benzoin
  powder
- 1 level teaspoon powdered
  allspice
- 100 drops rose oil (synthetic)

Essential oils:

- 80 drops bergamot
- 60 drops geranium
- 40 drops lavender
- 20 drops clary sage
- 2 crushed cinnamon sticks
- 30 g all spice berries
- 15 g whole cloves

dry method

one Place the dry ingredients in a large mixing bowl.

two Separately measure out the essential oils using a pipette and drip them into a small screw top bottle. Shake thoroughly to mix. Place ground spices and fixatives in a bowl and add a little of the oil blend, stirring to make a crumbly mix. Place the carrier materials in another bowl and add the remaining blended oils, mixing thoroughly to coat them. Cover and leave for at least 24 hours.

three Place the dried flowers in a mixing bowl and stir together with a wooden spoon. Add the carrier materials and mix; and then add the spicy mixture, thoroughly mixing until well distributed.

four Place in a lidded glass or china container (in a dark place if you have chosen glass) for at least 6 weeks to mature. (Avoid using plastic containers, which absorb fragrance or metal, which interferes with the scent.)

silica dried flowers

DENSELY PETALLED FLOWERS are beautiful when dried and are a great way to decorate a bowl of pot pourri. The most effective way to dry them is to use a desiccant that draws the moisture from the petals, leaving them perfectly intact and preserving much of their colour. Fine silver sand or borax (or a mixture of the two) can be used, but the most effective and easiest drying agent is silica. Cover the bottom of a lidded plastic box with 1.25 cm (½ in) of silica gel. Lay the flowers gently on top. Carefully fill the centre of the flowers with the gel, then build up around the flowers so that they are supported, before covering them completely. If there is room in the box, continue to layer the flowers until the top is reached. Replace the lid firmly and leave for between 3-5 days, depending on the size of the flowers. The gel will turn from blue to pink as it absorbs the moisture, indicating when the flowers are ready. Shake off any excess gel. The gel can be placed in a warm oven to dry off, regain its blue colour and be ready for use again.

scented smoke

NOT ALL SMOKE smells unpleasant, of course. An open fire can become a source of fantastically aromatic, evocative scents if fragrant woods, or indeed herbs, are burned. A richly scented pile of cedar or applewood logs heaped up by the fireplace adds fragrance to the air even before burning. Scented smoke wafting through the air is a powerful draw; smelling it in the open air urges you inside to the glow of the fire. Connotations of cosy, crumpet-toasting teatimes crowd in. Pine cones and fallen conifer twigs collected on autumn walks make excellent fragrant kindling, and bundles of herb prunings — bay, southernwood and rosemary — can add supplementary scents to an ebbing fire. The fragrant smoke from incense sticks gives a room an instant, contemplative atmosphere, and thoughtful display ideas can make the skinny sticks something of a decorative feature in their own right.

Wood must be allowed to dry properly in order to burn well and give a good fragrance, needing at least six months. Suitable hardwoods for the fire include oak, ash, poplar and cedar. Fruit and nut trees — pear, cherry, apple — can smell lovely, as can soft resinous woods such as pine and spruce. If you don't have access to a stock of fragrant wood, you can create your own by applying a single drop of essential oil on each log as you pile it up beside the fire — cedarwood, cypress, pine, sandalwood and juniper are good choices.

pine cones

GATHER AND KEEP pine cones in baskets by the fire. To enhance the smell, add a drop of pine essential oil to each cone, then seal them into an airtight plastic bag for a few days, or until you want to use them. Either use them to make the fireplace attractive and smell wonderful during the summer months, or keep them for Christmas, when they can be used as a table centrepiece or to decorate the fire surround. Simply add further drops of the essential oil as the aroma fades.

TOP LEFT: *Incense sticks, chosen from a host of different fragrances, fill a room with a distinctive smoky scent. Their leggy, minimal forms lend themselves well to contemporary interiors.*

TOP RIGHT: *Fill the room with the unmistakable zest of resinous pine by adding branches to your fire.*

BELOW LEFT: *A roaring fire makes a room instantly welcoming — warm in temperature and in mood. Burning fragrant woods like cedar, apple, pine, juniper and cherry adds immeasurably to the enjoyment.*

BELOW RIGHT: *Add a few drops of pine essential oil to dry pine cones collected on winter walks for additional fragrance, both on the fire and in an empty fireplace during the summer months.*

Aromatic Herbal Bundles

THE MEDIEVAL PRACTISE of tossing perfumed 'cakes' of dried herbs, petals, resins and bark onto the open fire to fill the room with fragrant smoke is the inspiration for these simple wraps of herbs. Store them in a open basket within easy reach of the fire for use whenever you want to enjoy their rich outdoor aroma. They are extremely simple to make, a pleasantly aromatic task that even children might like to share.

you will need

- Raffia, string, (any kind of natural twine that burns easily will do, but avoid plastic)
- Any abundant aromatic herbs — rosemary, bay, lavender, thyme, southernwood, lemon verbena, sage, eucalyptus. Use any trimmings from a pruning session. Make them up in the early autumn months, ready for the first open fires.

method

one Take a small handful of leaves, twigs or sprigs of the herbs. A mixture of all three will also work well.

two Take a single length of raffia and simply wind it around them firmly, securing with a simple slip knot at the end of the thread. Keep them in a basket beside the fireplace, and as the fire is beginning to die, throw one or two onto the gently burning embers, to release their fragrance.

herbs for soothing

BEDROOMS ARE PLACES of sanctuary and relaxation, so it is important to bring feelings of contentment to the fore. Essential oils of lavender, camomile, geranium, rose, ylang ylang, frankincense, jasmine, melissa or petitgrain — or indeed your own combination of any of these — will unwind the mind beautifully. They can be vaporized in a room spray or simply dropped onto a handkerchief tucked into your pillow. For an erotically charged environment, look to sandalwood, patchouli, rose, jasmine, ylang ylang and neroli. Rose petals have strong historic and folkloric connotations of sensuality and seduction, scattering them over the floor of bridal bedrooms being the traditional way of releasing their heady scent at the appropriate time. You could emulate this with a rose-based pot pourri, left to disperse its scent in open dishes or enclosed in fabric sachets and secreted around the room after the fashion the Romans set of incorporating rose petals into their upholstery.

ABOVE: *Incorporating fragrance into a decorative accessory, such as this bird mobile for a baby, using camomile, has many applications. The same idea can be adapted to make special soft toys for children or for pets — you could incorporate catmint in a feline toy. The idea will also work for pin cushions or rose-petal love-heart tokens for Valentine's Day.*

baby mobile

THE SOOTHING PROPERTIES of camomile are particularly suited to babies and can be helpful in cases of colic and when sleep patterns are disturbed — very weak infusions making the perfect drink to offer between feeds. Introducing the gentle scent of the herb to the nursery environment can have equally calming effects. We have filled bird-like shapes with dried camomile and lavender to make a decorative, fragrant mobile that sparkles as it swings gently above the cot.

Make up small muslin sachets in very simplified bird shapes and stuff them with equal amounts of lavender and camomile. These birds are finished by overlaying the basic sachet shapes with scraps of silk organza, stitched into place, complete with beaks and tails. To make them attractive for baby to watch, they are then decorated with eye-catching sparkly sequins.

A length of gold cord is threaded through the middle of each bird and they are simply attached to a basic mobile with clips. As they gently move around, drifts of soporific scent will calm your baby to sleep. An additional drop of camomile essential oil can simply be dropped on to each bird as the scent fades.

hot water bottle sachets

THAT MOST PROSAIC OF household objects, the humble hot water bottle, can become a thing of luxury if it is scented. A sachet full of fragrant ingredients, such as herbs — and particularly those that aid sleep or deter insects like mosquitoes — can be slipped inside a hot water bottle cover, the heat emanating from the bottle will intensify the aroma of the herbs in the sachet, producing something quite heady and soothing to inhale as you gently drop off to sleep.

LEFT: *Using remnants of gorgeous fabrics, like this letter from an old monogrammed linen sheet, will make these scented sachets to slip into hot water bottle covers extra special.*

one   two   three

Herbal Cushions

you will need

To make a 20 x 30 cm

(8 x 12 in) pillow:

• 25 g (1 oz) dried hops

• 25 g (1 oz) dried lavender

• 10 g (¼ oz) dried sweet

  woodruff

• Mixing bowl

• A little vodka

• Muslin or fine cotton

  fabric

• Decorative cover fabric

• Basic sewing kit

(Adjust the balance of

herbs to your taste — you

may prefer a smaller

amount of hops, adding

instead more lavender or

sweet woodruff.)

THE POWER OF HERBS to soothe and heal mind and body has long been recognized, and it is interesting to observe the role plant products play in contemporary treatments for diseases as diverse as cancer and multiple sclerosis. Before the advent of modern scientific procedures and drugs, physicians relied on herbal remedies entirely. The physicians attending the afflicted King George III successfully eased his chronic insomnia with a pillow stuffed with hops, known to sedate and relax the mind. This recipe combines hops with the sweetly perfumed lavender and sweet woodruff, which was once used to stuff mattresses and scent bedlinen, making a scented bed companion guaranteed to promote a good night's sleep.

method

one Measure out the hops and place in a mixing bowl.

two Remove any twiggy bits. Add the lavender and sweet marjoram to the mixing bowl. At this point, add a few drops of vodka to lessen the rustle of the hops. Mix well.

three Cut two pieces of muslin or fine cotton fabric 24 x 34 cm (9½ x 13½ in). Sew around three edges 2 cm (¾ in) from the edge. Use pinking shears to trim the seams to 1 cm (⅜ in). Invert the sachet and stuff with the herb mixture. Hand sew the open end together. Now make the decorative cushion cover to the same size as the herb sachet. The cover is made in exactly the same way, enclosing the herb sachet and hand stitching it closed. Or make it with a button or zip opening along the middle of the back side, so that the cover can be removed for washing.

scents for a bedroom

For a calming, romantic environment, choose rose, ylang ylang, jasmine, rose geranium, lavender and the seductive neroli.

scents for a sitting room

Pine, cedarwood, sandalwood, frankincense, juniper and clary sage are appropriate for relaxation.

scents for a home office

Try basil, rosemary and lavender for concentration.

peppermint pillows

MAKE COTTON SACHETS and fill them with a mixture of dried lavender, spearmint and peppermint in roughly equal portions, but adjust the proportions according to your taste. Slip them inside cushion covers used in the sitting room and their sweet, insect-repelling smell will be released as they are leant on. Experiment with other dried herbs mixed together, such as lemon verbena, lemon balm, scented geranium leaves, sweet woodruff and sweet marjoram.

pet pillow

MAKE SURE YOUR ANIMAL sleeps on a sweet-smelling bed. This mix is anti-flea and de-odorizing. How much of the mixture you use will depend on the size of the bag. You will need roughly 100 g (4 oz) for a 30 x 30 cm (12 x 12 in) sachet. Use 2 parts dried lavender, 1 part dried rue, 1 part dried peppermint (or try catmint if you are making the pet pillow for a cat, as they generally

LEFT: *Using ingredients that traditionally deter fleas within a scented sachet that can be zipped into the top panel of a pet's beanbag is a discreet and fragrant solution to a common problem. A mixture of lavender, rue, peppermint (or catmint which cats love) and pennyroyal works beautifully.*

love it), 1 part dried pennyroyal. The sachet is likely to be much larger than the sleep pillow, so to prevent all the herbs from falling into one section, fill the sachet in stages, sewing each section in like a quilt. For example, if the sachet is to be 50 x 50 cm (20 x 20 in), divide the mix into 5 equal amounts and stitch a seam every 10 cm (4 in). Finally, sew across the middle adjacent to the other lines of stitching. Slip the sachet into a square-shaped bean bag with a zipped cover.

• Keep fleas away by adding 1 drop of citronella or lemongrass essential oil to the shampoo each time you bathe your pet.

• To get rid of doggy smells, spray bedding regularly with a solution of 3 drops eucalyptus oil and 2 drops rosemary to 50 ml (2 fl oz) of purified water. This makes a quick, instant spray. As there is no alcohol to preserve the oils, make up small amounts at a time and shake the bottle vigorously before using.

These simple lavender
variations on the theme of
incense make a delightfully
understated centrepiece on an
outdoor table, where their
insecticide properties may
come in useful. They burn
quickly, so have plenty to
hand and be careful, as they
do tend to spark.

natural lavender sticks

DIP EACH LAVENDER STEM into a solution of 25 g (1 oz) saltpetre dissolved in 100 ml (3½ fl oz) warm water for half an hour. Once they have dried, stand them in a holder. It is best to burn a few at a time outside, where a gentle breeze will help them burn steadily, releasing a subtle aroma which will deter insects.

Think also about planting aromatic plants just outside the windows of the most lived-in rooms. On summer evenings when the day has cooled, especially after a shower of rain, the scents will waft through the open windows. Magnolia has a wonderful, sweet spicy smell; night-scented stocks can be almost overpowering if they have been drenched with sun during the day; and then, of course, there are all manner of scented roses.

candles

BELOW: Invest in a range of perfumed candles so that you can choose the fragrance to suit your mood. Their subtle variations in colour make a beautiful display.

THE ULTIMATE SEDUCTIVE ploy is, of course, the shameless application of candlelight. The flickering, flattering light turns the most prosaic of interiors into a shadowy, intimate space. Using scented candles exploits the twin sensual pleasures of fragrance and gentle lighting to the full, which explains their huge popularity. You can achieve your own moody atmosphere by simply adding a few drops of a favourite oil to the well of melted wax around the extinguished wick of a standard unscented candle. (NEVER do this when a candle is alight as the oils are flammable.) When relit, the fragrance will diffuse into the air. Another simple method is to spray the candle with your chosen blend of oils, or for a more permanent, stronger scent, mix a few drops of oil with one of benzoin or any other fixative and paint the mixture over the surface of the candle. Making your own scented candles isn't as complex as you might imagine and gives you the endless flexibility implicit in fragrancing with essential oils.

Scented Votive Candles

you will need

• 225 g (8 oz) paraffin wax or beeswax, available in granules (or old candles can be melted down — make sure they are clean before using and remove old wicks when melted).

• Wick (the thickness of the wick will depend on the thickness of the candle you plan to make. For an up to 5 cm (2 in) wide candle, use a small wick; for up to 10 cm (4 in) thick, use a medium size; for up to 15 cm (6 in), use a large wick

• Wick stabiliser

• Bain-marie

• Twig or pencil to hold the wick taut

• Glasses (look out for small glass night-light holders)

• Glue gun (optional)

• Scissors

• Essential oils, about 60 drops to 225 g (8 oz) wax

SCENTED CANDLES have been around since the eighteenth century, but have never been as popular as they are today. It is simple to make your own, scented exactly as you would wish using essential or perfume oils in a range of fragrances suited to different moods. Using small glass containers has practical as well as aesthetic advantages, since the candles can be positioned anywhere you wish without the risk of wax spilling on to delicate surfaces. Reposition the wick each time you extinguish a candle while the wax is still molten to ensure that it burns evenly down the glass. Follow the same recipe to make outdoor candles with the power to deter insects by adding the appropriate essential oils and pouring the melted wax into tiny terracotta pots or galvanized containers.

method

one Assemble all the ingredients and equipment before you begin

two Melt the wax slowly in the bain-marie over a low heat. Turn on glue gun to heat. Meanwhile, prepare the glass holders. Tie a length of wick to a twig with a simple knot. Pass the other end of the wick through a metal stabilizer and lie the twig across top of glass, keeping the wick taut. Cut the wick to length, leaving about 1 cm ($^3/_8$ in) excess. Now dip the length of the wick briefly in the melted wax and pull it straight. With a drop of heated glue from the gun, secure the metal stabilizer in the middle of the bottom of the glass. (Alternatively, pour a spoonful of wax into the bottom, and just before it sets position the stabilizer in the wax and allow to cool.) Make sure the wick stands straight up the middle by resting the twig across the top of the glass.

three Add drops of essential oil to the melted wax, having let it cool a little but before a skin forms. Stir in slowly, making sure air bubbles are not formed. Now pour into the glass holders carefully in two or three stages, allowing the wax to cool until it reaches to within about 1 cm ($^3/_8$ in) from the top. As it cools, a depression will form. Fill this with more wax. When the wax has completely hardened (you can stand it in cold water to speed the process), remove twig and trim the wick to about 1 cm ($^3/_8$ in) in length.

one

two

three

CHAPTER **5**

THE SCENTED BATHROOM

B A T H I N G   W A S   an important daily ritual and pleasure for the Ancient Egyptians, the Greeks and the Romans, of course, who raised it to a fine art. Our experience of bathing today is closer to that of these ancient civilizations than it is to the utilitarian, early twentieth-century world of draughty, plunge purgatory. Now that the bathroom is again the arena for private meditation and sensual indulgence, we are cleaner than we've ever been!

bathing

AS WE HAVE SEEN elsewhere in this book, different fragrances evoke different responses, and the bathroom is one room in which we experience the starkest contrasts. Soothing away the strains of the day in glorious isolation, immersed in deep, warm water and surrounded by candlelight, perhaps with a glass of wine within reach, is the height of hedonism. At the other end of the sensory scale, a bathroom is also a place of early morning vigour, where a refreshing blast from a power shower energizes you for the day. Adding fragrance to fit either mood in the form of bath oils, shower gels, soaps, body lotions, scented candles or vaporized essential oils simply magnifies the effect of both cleansing experiences. In addition, we all respond individually to perfumes in a different way, and therefore need to spend time finding the ones that suit us best. This is particularly the case in the bathroom, where we tend to be alone — with no need to accommodate the tastes of others — and intent on justified self-indulgence.

One of the simplest ways to introduce fragrance into the bathroom is with herbs and flowers. The steamy warmth of a bathroom tends to intensify the smell of any plant — indoor jasmine is a good choice of pot plant if your bathroom is sufficiently well-lit, for example — and actually adding flowerheads and fragrant leaves to your bathwater gently scents it, like a tisane. Use camomile or marigold flowers for a relaxing, Ophelia-like experience; rose petals reminiscent of the film *American Beauty* if romance and drama are on your mind. Tying a muslin bag full of herbs to the hot tap as you draw your bath fills the air with therapeutic scents. Use whatever you have a good supply of — pine, rosemary, camomile or mint, for example. For a warming and air-passage clearing winter bath, try substituting pieces of peeled fresh ginger for the herbs. Another simple,

BELOW: *Fragrant oils, soaps and rinses can be made very easily by using essential oils and natural herbs. Introduce fresh herbs to your bathroom, where the naturally humid environment will diffuse their fragrance fast. Similarly, the scent of flowers in a warm bathroom is always strong.*

ABOVE: *Tie a branch of fresh eucalyptus leaves beneath your shower head to release its revitalizing, head-clearing fragrance each time you turn on the hot tap.*

attractive idea is to tie a generous branch of invigorating eucalyptus leaves to your shower head: as the hot water flows, their scent is released.

The naturally humid environment of a bathroom is the perfect place to take an inhalation if you have a cold, and eucalyptus is one of the most powerful anti-bacterial decongestants. Add a few drops of eucalyptus or benzoin essential oil to a bowl of hot — not boiling — water and breathe in the fragrance. Essential oils work wonderfully dropped directly into the bathwater and swirled around, combining the therapeutic effects of vaporization and immediate skin contact. However, do check the usage warnings to ensure your preferred oil is suitable for this purpose. Eucalyptus, for instance, is highly stimulating, as well as decongestant, and its use in the bath could prove counterproductive.

Our ancient and keen bathers in Egypt added vegetal and potassium-based salts to bathwater to clean their bodies. The corrosive quality of such mineral baths demanded the use of nourishing post-immersion oils to protect the skin. The Romans, however, favoured the use of oil to clean the skin, massaging it into the body before scraping away the emerging impurities with a curious curved implement called a strigil.

Today's bath oils tend to work in tandem with your chosen soap, not instead of it, and are principally to be enjoyed for the fragrance they bring and their moisturizing properties. Bathing with oils leaves a fragrant surface residue on the skin, locking in moisture and supplying a wondrous sheen. Making your own from blends of vegetable carrier oils mixed with essential oils or infused with macerated herbs and flowerheads gives enormous scope for all kinds of aromatic inspiration. Linking the perfume of soaps and oils makes good sense, as too great a medley of smells can begin to tire and confuse the mind, and some do not mix well in any case.

bathing potions

oatmeal and lavender exfoliating bath bag

Mix a handful of medium-ground oat flakes with a handful of lavender. Place in a muslin drawstring bag (or cut a square of muslin, pile the ingredients in the middle and draw up the edges, tying with a length of string). The oatmeal will swell as it soaks in the water, so make sure the string is not pulled too tightly. Hang under the hot tap as the bath runs, then use the bag to gently rub the skin.

peppermint footbath

Dissolve a tablespoon of bicarbonate of soda in a bowl of hot water. Add 2 drops of peppermint essential oil or a handful of fresh mint. Soak feet for a good 10 minutes — or as long as you feel comfortable. Or use cool water instead.

rose geranium bath salts

Detoxifying sea salts and bicarbonate of soda have a cleansing and soothing effect on the skin. You will need:

• 100 g (4 oz) sea salt

• 100 g (4 oz) soda crystals

• 50 g (2 oz) bicarbonate of soda

• 40 drops rose geranium essential oil (or another that you may prefer).

Place all ingredients into a bowl, including essential oil, and mix well. Place the crystals in a screw top jar for a week, shaking from time to time. Use a generous handful in each bath.

scents for the bathroom

Uplifting bergamot, grapefruit and lime are ideal for morning ablutions, while relaxing rose, lavender and camomile are appropriate for the evenings.

fresh herbs to strew in the bath

Herbs can simply be strewn in the bathwater, or enclosed in a muslin bag suspended from the taps. Try rosemary; marigold as an astringent; bay; camomile for relaxation; scented geranium leaves; lavender flowers; roses; lemon verbena for scent; and pine needles for stimulating and decongesting. A tablespoon of finely ground oatmeal can be added to cleanse and soften the skin. Once the herbs have been exhausted, discard and rinse the bag with fresh water. Simply replenish the bag with a handful of fresh herbs (or 3 tablespoons of dried herbs).

ABOVE: *Scattering marigolds and rosemary into your bath is an aesthetic treat, as well as a soothing and fragrant experience for the body.*

BELOW LEFT: *Rose geranium bath salts, looking almost edible in a simple jar on a bathroom windowsill.*

one

two

Bath Oils

Vegetable oils:

- 70 ml (3 fl oz) sweet
  almond

- 20 ml (1 fl oz) apricot
  kernel

- 10 ml (½ fl oz)
  wheatgerm oil

Essential oils:

- 10 drops to 10 ml (½ fl oz)
  of vegetable oil.

BATHING WITH FRAGRANT OILS is a time-honoured sensual pleasure, combining the luxury of relaxing in hot water with the positive therapeutic benefits of vegetable and essential oils.

The scentless sweet almond oil used here is rich in proteins, minerals and vitamins that are good for all skin types. Apricot kernel oil is rich in minerals and vitamins and is especially good for sensitive and ageing skins. Wheatgerm is extremely nutritious, rich in vitamin E and a useful antioxidant, but not more than 10% should be used in a mixture of the base oils, because it might otherwise go rancid. Pour the bath oil mixture into a hot bath just before you get in, to reap the benefits of the essential oils before they evaporate. Soak yourself in the bath for at least 15 minutes — 30 if you can manage it, to get a really thorough skin treatment.

method

one Measure the vegetable oils into a measuring jug. Add your chosen essential oils and stir well.

two Pour the mixture into a clean bottle. Add about 1-2 teaspoons of bath oil diluted with a small glass of milk, which is soothing to the skin and will help disperse the oils in the water. Pour under the tap as you fill the bath.

rose body oil

Deliciously scented, smooth, light and slightly astringent, the oil can be used all over your body after a hot bath.

- 75 ml (3 fl oz) rose water
- 1 level teaspoon borax
- 2 tablespoons almond oil
- 1 tablespoon grapeseed oil
- 5 drops rose maroc (absolute)
- 5 drops rose geranium

Place rose water in a bain-marie, add the borax and slowly dissolve, then add the oils and whisk together. Take off the heat and add the essential oils. Pour into a sterilized bottle. Shake well before using.

ABOVE: *Natural soaps are a pleasure to use, touch and smell, particularly those with olive oil, which has a natural earthy aroma.*

body care

ADDING ESSENTIAL OILS to unfragranced liquid soap or shower gel transforms them instantly. Ring the changes with some devoted to refreshing the mind (bergamot, lemon, geranium, lavender or peppermint) and others to sensual sweetness (rose, sandalwood, jasmine or ylang ylang). Soap as we know it today is a relatively recent addition to bathroom life, invented in Europe in the Middle Ages. Deliciously scented, beautifully packaged soaps are available everywhere, so much so that the choice can become quite mesmerizing. Letting your creative juices flow to make your own, incorporating essential oils, herbs and spicy aromatics is hugely enjoyable. Alternatively, you can simply enclose a wad of cotton wool impregnated with a favourite essential oil in a sealed bag with a bar of unperfumed soap and leave it for about a month — by which time the scent will have permeated the soap.

herbal shampoo

Make up a strong herbal infusion. Try camomile or marigold for lightening hair; sage and rosemary as good all-round conditioners and for darkening hair; or lime flowers or catmint for scalp irritation. Mix equal amounts of the herbal infusion to a pure, unscented shampoo or baby shampoo. Alternatively, simply add a drop of essential oil to the amount of shampoo you intend to use, decanted into a small cup and mixed in thoroughly.

herbal and floral hair rinses

Make up a strong infusion to use as a final rinse when washing your hair. Place it in a bowl, pouring it over your head and allowing as much of your hair as possible to have a good soak.

To make up a strong rinse, infuse 2 tablespoons of dried herbs (or twice as much of fresh herbs) in 600 ml (1 pint) of mineral or spring water and slowly bring to the boil. Simmer for 5 minutes uncovered, then allow to cool with the lid on. Strain into a bowl.

cider vinegar herbal hair rinse

Cider vinegar is a very effective natural hair rinse for all types of hair, leaving it really shiny. Add herbs to increase the aromatic and therapeutic effect.

Take any size bottle of cider vinegar and remove about a one-third of the liquid. Add a good handful of fresh herbs — rosemary, lavender, lime flower, lemon verbena or rose geranium — and then fill up to the top of the bottle with the remaining cider vinegar. Replace the bottle top and store in a warm place, such as a sunny window-sill, for a couple of weeks, shaking daily. Strain the herbs out and discard, and repeat the procedure once or twice until you have attained the level of fragrance you require.

Simply add half a cupful to a basin of warm water and soak the hair as a final rinse.

nourishing lavender cream for hard-working hands

- 20 g (³/₄ oz) beeswax
- 20 g (³/₄ oz) cocoa butter
- 50 ml (2 fl oz) sweet almond oil
- 10 drops lavender essential oil

Place the beeswax, almond oil and cocoa butter in a bain-marie and gently dissolve together. Remove from the heat and stir the creamy mixture well. Add the essential oil, mixing well. Store in a screw-topped container.

one   two   three

Frankincense & Myrrh Soap Balls

MAKING YOUR OWN SOAP is a fairly lengthy and complicated process that requires some practice. This is a very simple way of introducing your favourite smells to a basic, fragrance-free soap, using a combination of nourishing vegetable oil, oatmeal as a natural exfoliant and healing and nourishing honey. The soaps are scented with the heavenly combination of frankincense and myrrh. The spicy, woody scent of frankincense is uplifting, whilst the balsamic, musty scent of myrrh is known to be anti-fungal and healing. Try any of the following essential oils as an alternative: mandarin, clove, cinnamon leaf, benzoin or lavender.

An additional tablespoon of ground or finely chopped dried herbs will add texture.

- 250 g (9 oz) pure, un-scented soap — the best quality you can find.
- 125 ml (4 fl oz) water
- 1 tablespoon honey
- 1 tablespoon finely ground oatmeal
- 1 teaspoon sweet almond oil or apricot kernel oil
- 12 drops myrrh essential oil
- 8 drops frankincense essential oil
- cheese grater
- bain-marie
- wooden spoon

method

one Grate the soap with a fine cheese grater.

two Place the soap in the bain-marie with the water. Gently heat over a low heat. Gradually the mixture will form a thick and fairly sticky paste. When the soap has melted, add the honey, oatmeal and oil and dried herbs (optional) and mix in well. Transfer to a clean bowl and then add in the essential oils. Mix very thoroughly.

three Have a bowl of water to hand and wet your hands. Now take a small handful of the mixture and mould into around balls. You will be able to make approximately 2 large balls or 5 or so smaller ones. Place on a sheet of grease-proof paper and leave to harden for a week of so. Alternatively, put the finished mixture in a shaped mould, lining the inside with greaseproof paper. Any small carton will do, such as a cut-down fruit juice carton for a square shape.

one   two   three

Eau de Cologne

you will need

- 70 ml (3 fl oz) vodka
- Lime rind
- Lemon rind
- 2 cardamom pods
- 30 ml (1½ fl oz) purified water
- Water filter
- Filter paper
- Jug
- Sterilized bottles or jars — use dark glass bottles to preserve the perfume

Essential oils:

- 20 drops bergamot
- 10 drops lemon
- 5 drops rose geranium
- 10 drops sweet orange
- 5 drops orange
- 3 drops lavender
- 2 drops rosemary
- 1 drop clove

CREATE YOUR OWN simple eau de cologne by using essential oils, alcohol and water to open a whole new world of fragrance. This recipe is traditional, relying on citrus notes for a light and refreshing cologne to splash on liberally throughout the day. Ideally, pharmaceutical alcohol should be used, but it is not possible to buy it in Britain without a license. Vodka, being the least scented easily available alcohol, is best to use, making sure that you buy as high a proof as possible.

To make an aromatic after shave, use the same basic eau de cologne recipe. For a more masculine scent, use the following mix of essential oils: 10 drops lavender; 10 drops bergamot; 8 drops frankincense; 5 drops mandarin; 5 drops grapefruit; 5 drops lime; 3 drops black pepper. Mix the essential oils and leave for 48 hours. Place a stick of cinnamon and a scraping of nutmeg in the alcohol, and also leave for 48 hours. Filter the liquid, add about half as much again of witch hazel and shake well. Finally, add about the same amount of orange flower water and shake. Combine with the essential oils mixture, store in a dark bottle and leave for 4-6 weeks.

method

one Measure the essential oils together in a sterilized bottle. Swirl to mix and leave to mature for 48 hours.

two Place crushed cardamom pods and a 5 cm (2 in) rind of lemon and orange into another bottle with the vodka and leave for 48 hours.

three Filter the alcohol and add to the essential oils, swirling together so they are well mixed. Leave for another 24 hours. Finally, add the purified water. Store in a dark glass bottle and allow to mature for at least 6 weeks.

CHAPTER 6

CELEBRATIONS

TIMES OF CELEBRATION — weddings, christenings, birthday parties — are

those we love to recall, and often the trigger for remembrance is a particular fragrance. It might be the smell of

crushed rose petal confetti, spiced wine from a winter party or the sweet warmth of resinous pine at Christmas.

Fragrance on special occasions has a dual role — immediate sensory enjoyment and stored memory.

evoking an atmosphere

A FANTASTIC RANGE of fragrances surrounds every great social occasion: the smell of cooking wafting through the house or of barbecue smoke seeping in from the garden; the sweet odour of wines or celebration punch; the intermingling of people's perfumes and aftershaves; the heady scent of luxuriant floral arrangements; and the unique aroma of excited children, tearing about the place. But before your party gets in full swing, there are a number of ways to lay the foundations for a truly special scented celebration.

Bring plenty of fresh seasonal flowers, fruits and herbs inside, and don't just limit their use to the principal party rooms. A fragrant posy, combining herbs and flowers, in the bathroom, or in a bedroom where guests may be leaving their coats, gives real pleasure. Evergreens and richly coloured berries are perfect for decorating winter parties, the smell of pine, spruce, eucalyptus, rosemary or bay leaves being just as pleasurable as the summer scents. A pile of unadorned oranges or tangerines interspersed with fresh bay leaves makes a simple, highly fragrant decoration that can be slowly dismantled and eaten. More intensely fragrant citrus decorations come in the shape of clove-studded pomanders, perhaps the most traditional of all seasonal purveyors of scent, that evoke the days when pomanders were considered vital weapons in the war against the stench of the Elizabethan peasantry.

Floral garlands in the spirit of Hawaiian leis and the wonderful, fragrant necklaces associated with Buddhist and Muslim religious celebrations make delightful embellishments for birthday parties — draped around the birthday girl's neck as a sign of special importance or on mantelpieces, chair backs and on tables. Use carnations, marigolds, daisies, stephanotis or tuberose. The folk tradition of decorating chairs for birthday celebrations or wedding festivities (thrones for bride and groom) with herbs, flowers and ribbons is a lovely one to follow, combining fragrance and colour in a really special way.

OPPOSITE: *Ring the changes by using a clipped bay tree at Christmas instead of the more predictable pine. Small pomanders tied to the branches have added fragrant appeal, while presents and other decorations are stacked up at the tree base in the usual way.*

You can make your rooms smell delicious in other ways, too. Make sure that there's plenty of freshly scented pot pourri in wide, beautiful dishes. For an evening party, position scented candles around the house (though its best to reserve the unfragranced variety for use on dining tables) and add drops of essential oils to light-bulb rings or vaporizers to fill the air with perfume and make your guests feel at ease. Heap the fireside with fragrant wood to feed the flames on winter nights. Outdoor parties need protection from biting insects, so position candles fragranced with insecticide oils on tables or in lanterns hung from trees, and keep a natural insecticide spray to hand. Drop woody herbs like rosemary and thyme on the barbecue for deliciously scented smoke.

ABOVE: *This is someone special's throne for a day, decorated with fresh flowers and set ready with an enticing present.*

OPPOSITE: *The subtle scent of spices seems particularly appropriate for winter celebrations — warming and comforting in the cold, with heartening associations of sunshine.*

birthday chair

TIE FRAGRANT ROSES or posies of fresh aromatic herbs to lengths of colourful raffia and use them to decorate a chair for someone special. The occasion could be a birthday, a wedding day or possibly a special anniversary.

spice necklaces

NECKLACES MADE FROM spices are fun, enduring and wonderfully aromatic to wear. The easiest spices to work with are those suggested here. Nutmegs will need to be drilled with a fine modelling drill bit. Place each one in a clamp before drilling. Thread them with a length of rustic string, knotting at even spaces in between each nutmeg. Allow each nutmeg some movement, as this releases the subtle aroma. You can rub down the surface of each nutmeg with fine sandpaper to

RIGHT: *Threading fresh, scented flowerheads, such as these carnations, onto a length of string makes a beautiful decorative garland to wear or to drape.*

OPPOSITE TOP: *Combine a variety of different lengths of spice necklace for an attractive aromatic display, hung here over delicate fabric.*

OPPOSITE CENTRE: *The hollow, quill-like sections of cinnamon bark lend themselves perfectly to threading to make tiny but powerful stringed garlands.*

OPPOSITE BOTTOM: *Fresh rosemary — tied into little bunches with thread — is all that is needed to bring appetizing aromas to the special meal table.*

reveal the attractive markings. To make the nutmegs go further and the necklace less heavy, try adding some beads to knot between them. Cinnamon is also suitable, but you need to cut the cinnamon sticks into equal lengths, and then use a sharp and heavy needle to thread the string up through the middle of each stick. It is best to avoid those that are too flaky, as they will probably fall apart as you try to thread them. Cardamoms can be threaded on a fine, strong linen thread. You will need a fairly fine, sharp needle to thread up through the middle of each pod. The subtle perfumes of these spices drifts through the atmosphere wherever the necklaces are hung and they can be refreshed by holding them in a little steam over a kettle or pan of water. The spices can be rubbed with a little vaseline to bring out their rich colours.

spice beads

MIX TOGETHER about 50 g (2 oz) of powdered spices, such as cinnamon, clove or star anise, including orris root as a fixative. Mix with 75 g (3 oz) of powdered gum benzoin and about 40 ml (1½ fl oz) of glycerine. Then add drops of essential oil. Try a blend of 5 drops of mandarin, 3 drops of cinnamon and 2 drops of benzoin. Roll out a little of the paste into bead shapes and place them somewhere warm to dry out. When they are beginning to dry, thread through the middle with a thick needle onto a length of strong linen thread or fine cord.

flower and herb garlands

Fresh flowers can also be made up into garlands to wear or to string up around a room. Any of the following are particularly lovely: sweet smelling carnations; tuberoses; marigolds; hyacinth flowerheads; lavender flowerheads (joined together as you would for a daisy-chain); bay leaves.

small herbed initials

Individual place settings can be marked with the aromatic initial of each guest for a festive meal. Simply bend a length of thick wire into the letter required, secure sprigs of mixed herbs using florist's wire, working from one end to the other.

m u l l e d   w i n e

c o r d i a l

• 5 cm (2 in) cinnamon stick

• 2 star anise

• 5 cloves

• 2 blades of mace

• 3 allspice berries

• A couple twists of orange zest

• A couple twists of lemon zest

• 1 bottle full-bodied red wine

• About 3 tablespoons caster
   sugar or honey (to taste)

• A generous splash of fruit
   liqueur (optional)

Place all the ingredients (except
sugar) in a pan and heat very
slowly, without boiling, for 15
minutes. Add sugar, stirring to
dissolve. Adjust amount to
taste. Serve warm.

WINTER IS THE SEASON associated most powerfully with expectations of festivity and the giving and receiving of presents. The celebrations of Halloween, Thanksgiving, Christmas and New Year fall at a time of year when nature is doing its utmost to persuade us not to feel full of good cheer — it is cold and dark and nothing much seems to be happening in our gardens or hedgerows.

The result is that all the sensory associations of winter conspire to put us in the mood for celebration — a fall of snow, a black starlit night or a spectacular vermillion autumn sunset encourage us to toast crumpets by the fire and to savour rich, hearty stews and indulgent puddings. Once the celebrations are actually under way, the fragrances intensify even more as the traditional battery of herbs, fruits and spices is brought into play.

Supplement the earthy fragrance of pumpkin and squash that fills the air at Halloween with the sweeter notes of apples and quinces, left to ripen in dishes left in the warmth of your winter home. Embrace nostalgia by making toffee apples for consumption by the bonfire, and bury oiled and salted potatoes wrapped in silver foil in the hottest part of the fire. Make your Thanksgiving or Christmas turkey aromatic with fragrant herbs and spiced stuffings. Add zest to cranberry sauce with citrus fruit and customize mincemeat and Christmas pudding with exotic dried fruits and fortified wines.

There's almost nothing about Christmas that isn't aromatic, but it goes without saying that you can always make the experience more intense. Hang homemade pomanders around the house; bring bay trees in from the cold to act as supplementary Christmas trees; thread gingerbread cookies with ribbon as authentic continental tree decorations; perfume your candles with traditional oils of frankincense and myrrh; burn frankincense resin or vaporize spices in water over a burner to supplement the delicious environmental scents.

Citrus Pomanders

*Small unwaxed oranges —
Seville are best as they are less
juicy and more fragrant, or use
clementines, lemons, limes or
kumquats.*

- 25 g (1 oz) whole cloves for
  each fruit
- Wooden skewers
- Paring knife
- Equal amounts of ground
  orris root and mixed spice.

ORIGINALLY PIERCED BALLS of silver, gold or ceramic containing a mix of highly fragrant spices were used by the nobility to protect themselves from fetid stenches. A citrus version, studded with cloves and rolled in a mix of spices, was slightly less exclusive. Nowadays, its richly spicy long-lasting fragrance makes it particularly lovely to have around the home.

method

one Scrub the fruit clean and dry.

two With the paring knife, carefully score a pattern around — a spiral design or a segmented one, working from one end to the other. Prick the flesh carefully and evenly along the pared lines using the wooden skewer. Only prick 5-6 holes at a time, as they soon close up and it may be difficult to spot them.

three Insert the whole cloves into the holes As the fruit dries, it will shrink slightly, bringing the cloves a little closer together, so make sure not to pack them too tight. Insert the cloves in neat lines and spaced evenly apart. Place the finished fruit in a warm, dry place, such as an airing cupboard, for about a month, turning it from time to time.

Traditional pomanders need to be completely rolled in a bowl full of the spice mixture. It is a good idea to wear plastic or rubber gloves, as it is a rather messy procedure. Place onto kitchen paper and leave to dry as before for 6-8 weeks. If you intend to hang the pomanders from a tree, piece the fruit before you start to insert the cloves with a long wooden skewer from one end to the other. Remove once the pomanders have dried. Use the channel and a needle to pass through a long thread.

Cardamom Pomanders

one

two

you will

need

- Oblong blocks of florists'
  oasis
- Small sharp kitchen knife
- Glue gun
- Cardamom seeds — as fresh
  as possible, that is greenish,
  not pale and brittle
  Small twig with a leaf (bay
  will work well)

THE SPICY SWEET SCENT of the cardamom powerfully evokes all the colour and aromatic intensity of the Far East. Make the most of this spice's intensity by including the pods in mixed pot pourris or simply placing them in a bowl, slightly crushed so that people can sift their fingers through, releasing their scent as they pass. Their structure also lends itself well to decorative ideas such as covering these sculptured pear shapes. They make a beautiful still life for a table decoration or they can be artfully placed around the house during festive times.

method

one Carve out your pear shape from the oasis, using the kitchen knife. Remember that no two pears look alike. If you are making more than one, the display will look better if they are slightly different sizes.

two Warm the glue gun. Now smear a line of glue from the top of the pear to the bottom. Push the end of a cardamom seed into the sticky oasis, continuing along the line so that the seeds lie close and evenly. Continue until the pear is covered, leaving a small space at the top end to secure a twig with a leaf — a sprig of bay would be perfect.

ABOVE: *An updated version of the traditional hamper; it comprises a package of scented goodies, wrapped in cellophane, in a contemporary wire basket.*

FRAGRANCE, WHETHER in the shape of a simple bunch of flowers or an extravagant bottle of Chanel No 5, is always a welcome gift. It has always had associations of luxury and self-indulgence, implicit in the enjoyment of perfume making, and the recipient feels truly spoiled. When we give someone a scented gift, we're appealing to a deep, sensual instinct, so getting the fragrance right is important. All the ideas discussed in this book make wonderful presents — candles, bath oils, pot pourri — but take time to adapt the smells you choose to the personality of whoever you plan to surprise. Woody, citrus smells tend to appeal more to men than women, while a heady floral smell, based predominantly on rose or jasmine, is likely to find favour with your most feminine friends. Tread carefully if you know someone is particularly fussy, and spoil them instead with ideas they may not have thought of, like an incense mix or herbal sleep pillow. The beauty of natural fragrances is that if you keep your combinations simple, it's very hard to produce anything really offensive to anyone.

Once you've made your selection of scented goodies, think of imaginative ways to present them. Perfumed papers make the act of wrapping as enjoyable as that of unwrapping and can be made in much the same way as scented drawer liners. Choose ribbons in translucent silks or sprightly patterns, or keep the look earthy with natural raffia or string. Putting together a selection of items in a basket is a lovely, generous idea. In addition to traditional woven baskets, small garden trugs are ideal for the purpose. Posies of fresh flowers and herbs tied on to gift baskets give them extra appeal.

heavenly hamper

ONE OF THE BEST and truly original gifts to receive must be a selection of lovingly homemade scented goodies. Look out for unusual baskets to arrange the items in. Here a wire basket lined with a generous sheet of transparent cellophane holds a selection of scented oils, lavender water, pot pourri, pomanders and a small bottle of eau de cologne. The cellophane is gathered up and tied with a piece of string, which is then adorned with a leafy bay garland. When the cellophane is untied, there will be the immediate, delicious pungency of the pomanders. Another way of creating an aromatic impact is to scatter a little pot pourri or place a scented card and envelope inside the gift. Label the products and include any specific instructions the recipient may need to know. Either glue hand-written labels onto the product or tie them on with string. For a modern look, use computer-printed labels tied on with a length of fuse wire. If you are printing from a computer, strengthen and protect the paper with transparent adhesive tape on both sides. Pierce through the label with the end of the fuse wire or use a hole punch — simple, quick and effective.

a gift of gold frankincense and myrrh

THE DEEP, LONG-LASTING smoky aroma of frankincense and myrrh is altogether calming, inspiring and uplifting. Pack together the two resins or a bottle of each essential oil and place in a small box covered with gold leaf for an inspired gift for Christmas. Traditionally, 3 parts frankincense are combined with 1 part myrrh.

christmas room spray

Essential oils:
- 5 drops cedarwood
- 3 drops mandarin
- 1 drop clove
- 1 drop bay
- 25 ml (1 fl oz) 90% proof vodka
- 50 ml (2 fl oz) purified water.

Add the essential oils to the vodka and leave for 24 hours. Add the purified water. Store in an atomizer bottle. Experiment with citrus oils: pine, sandalwood, cypress, cedarwood, cinnamon, clove, bay, frankincense and myrrh.

one

two

Scented Paper

you will need

- Sheets of paper, cards or envelopes for scenting.
- Sheet of blotting paper as large as the wrapping paper; or use two pieces.
- Roll of cellophane
- Adhesive tape
- Synthetic rose oil

For paper decorations and pot pourris, there is really no point in using costly essential rose oils, so use one of the excellent synthetics. Use about 15 drops for large sheets of wrapping paper.

FOR A REALLY UNIQUE PRESENT that is as pleasurable to wrap as it is to undo, use scented paper. It will make a humble present something really special. Incorporate the dried leaves or petals of the scent that you have chosen, trapping them by an outer layer of cellophane. Choose the scent of rose and a scattering of rose petals as a symbol of your love, recalling the days when flowers had their own language. Different plants were known to symbolize particular qualities or emotions: basil and rose for love; camomile for patience; lavender for silence; marjoram for happiness; mint for wisdom and purity; sage for glory; and violet for faithfulness.

method

one Apply the essential oils in drops evenly distributed over the blotting paper. This is done so that the wrapping or writing papers absorb the scent within an airtight enclosure. If the oils are dropped directly onto your papers, unsightly stains will occur.

two If you are scenting a couple of pieces of wrapping paper, place the blotting paper in between them. Now place the papers on top of a sheet of cellophane that is larger than the papers (you can always cut two pieces of cellophane and tape them together to create a really big sheet). Roll them up, together with any envelopes or cards that you want to include. Use adhesive tape to secure them, making sure that the cellophane is folded in at each end, sealing the papers. Leave for a couple of days — a week if possible.

aromatic foods

THE ENJOYMENT OF EATING together provides a focus and structure for any event, from the simplest weekend picnic to the most elaborate Christmas feast. Making the most of food doesn't necessarily mean making it look particularly striking, although taking trouble with presentation is always appreciated. If you can introduce distinctive aromatic elements to your party food, your guests will remember it with longing.

There is nothing complicated about doing this — just a little forethought and preparation are required. Look to your herbs. Whatever you cook will be the better for them, and any cold food will be dramatically enhanced with the addition of a few fragrant leaves: chicken with coriander, tarragon, thyme or basil; lamb with mint; fish with parsley or dill. Garnishing plates with complementary herbs is always successful, and adding them to salads makes something special of an everyday dish. Try mint with sliced tomatoes as a change from basil (it's delicious in white bread sandwiches, too) or add a few leaves to a fruit salad or to piles of strawberries and cream. Sometimes flowers can bring their aromatic delicacy to bear on food, and their petals can be used as garnish.

homemade mincemeat

The heavenly smell of spicy mincemeat pies cooking in the oven or warming over the wood burning stove is quintessential Christmas, inspiring family and friends to gather together to decorate the house. Somehow, Christmas Eve would not feel right without this essential kitchen aroma

- 225 g (8 oz) cooking apples, chopped
- 100 g (4 oz) beef (or vegetarian) suet
- 100 g (4 oz) raisins
- 100 g (4 oz) currants
- 50 g (2 oz) cherries
- 50 g (2 oz) dried apricots
- 50 g (2 oz) prunes
- 100 g (4 oz) candied peel

- 50 g (2 oz) slivered almonds
- grated zest and juice of 1 orange and 1 lemon (unwaxed)
- 175 g (6 oz) soft dark sugar
- 2 teaspoons mixed spice
- 1 teaspoon ground cinnamon
- 1 teaspoon ground nutmeg
- 3 tablespoons brandy

Mix all ingredients (except brandy) well and leave for 24 hours, covered with a clean cloth. Cook at 140°C/gas 1 for 2 hours, covering top with foil. Cool, stirring occasionally. When cold, add brandy and store in sterilized jars, with wax discs and airtight lid. Keep in a cool, dark cupboard.

mint julep

A delicious combination of whisky and mint is an old favourite — perfect for hot summer evenings.

- 1 measure whisky per glass
- 2 or 3 mint leaves per glass
- 1 teaspoon sugar per glass
- Crushed ice to half fill the glass
- Mint leaves to decorate.

Put ice cubes into a clean plastic bag and crush them with a rolling pin. Place the crushed ice in whisky glasses. Add sugar and roughly shredded or crushed mint leaves to each glass. Pour over the whisky and stir well to mix the julep. Decorate each glass with a sprig of mint leaves.

elderflower cordial

This cordial encapsulates the aroma of an early summer when the hedgerows are bursting with blossom. It is simply gorgeous iced, with fizzy water and perhaps a splash of gin.

- 25 good-sized elderflower heads
- 1.5 kg (3 lbs) sugar

- 4 unwaxed lemons, scrubbed
- 60 g (2½ oz) tartaric acid or citric acid
- 1 litre (2 pints) water

Gather 25 elderflower heads in full bloom. Strip off the bigger stems and shake off any bugs, then place them in a large bowl. Dissolve the sugar with the water in a pan. Pour over the elderflowers and add the sliced lemons and the tartaric acid. Leave for 24 hours with a clean cloth over the top. Line a sieve with a double layer of fine muslin and strain into a clean jug. Decant into sterilized bottles and store in a cool dark place.

picking drying & storing herbs & flowers

WHILE THERE IS LITTLE doubt that fresh herbs and flowers are preferable, drying gives you the freedom to use them whenever you like, not just in season. Dried correctly, their colour, smell, taste and healing properties will be largely preserved. The principle requirements are shade, good ventilation and warmth.

Harvest leaves and stems when herbs are young and leafy, before flowering begins; flowers when the plants are in full bloom; and seeds when pods begin to turn yellow or brown. Choose a dry day and pick early, before the sun heats up but after the dew has gone. Handle the herbs carefully to avoid bruising the leaves. It's best to leave most leaves, except perhaps the largest, in sprigs. Discard any weeds, discoloured or damaged leaves and wash the remainder in cool water. Gently cut off flowerheads like marigold or camomile.

Spread the herbs out in a single layer across flat, shallow containers or, ideally, on cheesecloth or muslin frames that allow air to circulate. A layer of newspaper or wrapping paper makes a good drying surface. Place the containers in a dry, warm and airy place away from sunlight — an attic or shed is ideal, or an airing cupboard if there is ventilation. Leave for at least 4 days, turning the leaves once a day.

Alternatively, strip off the lower leaves of any sprigs and tie together in bunches. Suspend these upside down in a shaded, dry, warm and airy place. Make sure they hang away from the wall — an old-fashioned clothes airer is ideal. While it is possible to speed things up by using a cool oven or hanging them in front of a fire, it does reduce their aroma.

Herbs should only be stored for long periods when they are completely dry. Leaves should be papery and brittle to the touch; stems and stalks should break easily, not bend; and petals should rustle but not crumble. Store them in clear glass containers for a week and look for any signs of moisture. If there is, turn them out and dry for a little longer. Fine-leaved herbs like rosemary and thyme are best stored in whole sprigs, and the leaves crumbled when they are to be used. Larger leaves should be crumbled and stored in small, opaque glass containers; store clear jars in a dark cupboard. Seal and label immediately. You could make up muslin bags of bouquet garnis at this stage and store them in a kilner jar.

Flowers and seedheads can be dried in the same ways. Once the seedheads or pods are dry, rub them to release the seeds; doing this outside allows the chaff to blow away. Dry the seeds for a further week, stirring them daily. Check for moisture before storing like the herbs.

Some evergreen herbs like dill and chives, and species with delicate leaves like parsley and chervil, are not suited to drying, but freezing for culinary use is an excellent option.

essential oils safety

ESSENTIAL OILS ARE invaluable for home fragrancing, and once you are acquainted with them in all their exquisite variety, you'll wonder how you ever managed without them. But, and it's a big but, they are highly potent substances and should be treated with care. Always read the label listing any precautions on your essential oils. Some are toxic; some sensitize the skin when they come into contact with sunlight; others should be avoided during pregnancy. Some, like peppermint and camphor, are considered incompatible with homoeopathic medicines and should only be taken internally if prescribed by a qualified aromatherapist. Those with epilepsy, high blood pressure and asthma should avoid using many essential oils. Children under 18 months old should never be treated with them.

Essential oils should be stored in dark, airtight glass bottles away from heat and out of the reach of children. Properly stored oils should last for around two years without significant deterioration. Most oils should only be used when diluted in a carrier oil (almond, grapeseed, jojoba or olive) before application to the skin. The total amount should never exceed 3% of the final volume. For example, 54-60 drops in a 100 ml (3½ fl oz) bottle of carrier oil amounts to about 3% of the total volume.

It's worth investing in accurate measuring equipment for ease and for safety. Ask your pharmacist for a glass dropper for measuring amounts very small amounts and a glass beaker or syringe to accurately measure larger amounts. A set of measuring spoons is also a useful back-up.

Use the best oils available from a reputable supplier. Synthetic and compounded oils don't have the therapeutic properties of true essential oils and some labelling can be misleading. It is best to buy your oils through an established retailer. Cost is a good indicator of quality for the very precious rose, neroli and jasmine oils; if they are priced equally with lavender, geranium and rosemary, for instance, they cannot be pure oils.

using oils

Be guided by your personal instincts when it comes to choosing essential oils for the home. The two major uses of the oils generally around the home are as air fresheners and for bathing. To make up scented air fresheners, add a 5-10 drops of essential oils to 50ml (2 fl oz) water in a spray, or diffuse the drops from burners, light-bulb rings or electric diffusers. For bathing, allow up to 8 drops per teaspoonful of base oil swished through the bathwater.

index

acknowledgments

FIRSTLY, THANKS MUST GO TO **Susan** for giving me the chance to work on this book and for providing plenty of support and encouragement. Special thanks to **Emma** for writing such intelligent and inspired text and for being my close ally and friend; to **Debi** for her beautiful, atmospheric photographs and good company and, of course, her team of wonderful assistants; to **Debbie** for her inspired design; and **Janet** for patiently providing so much assistance.

Finally to **Gum, Arthur** and **Madeleine** who have, as ever, endured and provided loving support when most needed; and are getting used to living in a scented home!

I would like to thank the following shops for kindly lending me their products: p. 2 Starfish with joss sticks - **story** • p. 9 Wood cheese mould - **story** • p. 62-63 wood block - **Twelve Mailorder** • p. 68 hops - **The Hop Shop** • p. 76 Twig photographs - **Debi Treloar** • p. 81 Hot water bottle cover - **Mint** • p. 84 Ticking chair - **Pimpernel Antiques** • p. 85 Fabric - **Celia Birtwell** • p. 86 Incense holders - **Mint**; lavender sticks idea, with thanks to **Homes and Gardens Magazine** • p. 87 Scented votives - **L'Artisan Parfumeur** • p. 104-105 Glass balls - **David Wainwright**; Cinnamon necklace - **story** • p. 115 Papier-mache plate - **Mint** • p. 116 Cardamon pears - idea by **Milla & Mone**, with thanks to Homes and Gardens

story 0207 377 0313 • **Twelve mailorder** 0207 6860773 • **Mint** 0207 224 4406 • **L,artisan Parfumeur** 0207 352 4196 • **Milla & Mone** 0207 263 6751 • **David Wainwright** 0207 431 5900 • **Pimpernel Antiques** 0207 731 2448 • **Celia Birtwell** 0207 221 0877